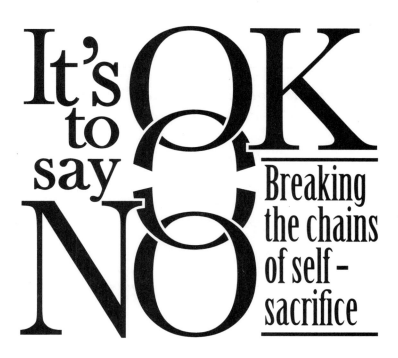

It's OK to say NO

Breaking the chains of self-sacrifice

Donald G. Smith

Books by Donald G. Smith

How to Cure Yourself of Positive Thinking
(Pocket Books)

The Joy of Negative Thinking
(Delancey Press)

People I Could Do Without
(White-Boucke Publishing)

Common Sense for the Beginner
(Waltsan Publishing)

Now Hear This
(Waltsan Publishing)

It's OK to Say NO
(WindRiver Publishing)

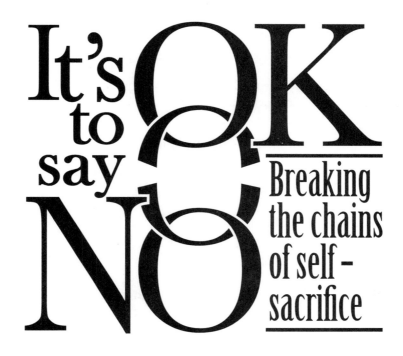

It's OK to say NO

OK
Breaking
the chains
of self-
sacrifice

Donald G. Smith

WindRiver Publishing, Inc.
Silverton, Idaho

WindRiver
Publishing

Queries, comments or correspondence concerning this work should be directed to the author and submitted to WindRiver Publishing at:

Authors@WindRiverPublishing.com

Information regarding this work or other works published by WindRiver Publishing, Inc., and instructions for submitting manuscripts for review for publication, can be found at:

www.WindRiverPublishing.com

Portions of this book were originally published in *The Joy of Negative Thinking*, ISBN 0-962793-56-6 (Delancey Press).

Library of Congress Control Number: 2005925289
ISBN-13 978-1-886249-29-5
ISBN-10 1-886249-29-6

First Printing 2005

Printed in the U.S.A. by Malloy, Inc., on acid-free paper

Table of Contents

Breaking the Chains of Self-Sacrifice

Let's start with this premise: the world is essentially a good place, people are essentially friendly, and life is good.

Assuming this to be true, we must then ask ourselves why there is so much unhappiness in the world, so much misery and injustice? The answer is easy. It's because we *allow* it to happen. We let the serpents into the garden when they have no business being there.

Happiness is not a tangible thing that we seek as though it were the Holy Grail. Happiness is nothing more than the absence of unhappiness, which means that if we can get rid of all the disruptive elements in our lives—things, situations, people—we can achieve the norm: which is happiness. The big advantage is that we're working with a sliding scale, so we don't have to face an all-or-nothing proposition. If we drive only half of the snakes from the garden then we are 50% better off than we were, and 90% is sheer bliss—far better than any of us can hope to expect.

The point is, we have a choice—we can choose to live happily or choose to live unhappily. Personally, I believe that given the choice, it is better for me to give up something I want than to have something thrust on me that I don't want. For example, I would give up lobster to avoid eating Spam; I would give up a free trip to the Bahamas to avoid a three-day orgy watching someone else's vacation slides; or I would gladly give up an evening with good friends if it meant avoiding a corresponding session with ignorant louts.

As you can see from my examples, the choice I'm talking about is whether or not to permit myself to make an unreasonable or ignoble sacrifice in order to accommodate someone else—especially if that person is undeserving. We're taught from a young age that self-sacrifice is good, noble, and honorable—and it can be. What we're not told is that self-sacrifice is a very valuable commodity that should be treasured and not be wasted on trivial matters. Most of the unhappiness in our lives is often a result of willingly sacrificing ourselves, our time, or our money for causes or reasons that don't deserve it.

Making a definitive choice to sacrifice ourselves sparingly is truly the secret of happiness. The funny thing is, people almost never trade something they really want to avoid something they really don't want. If we diagnose this problem, we'll find such symptoms as indecisiveness, a desire to avoid conflict, the inability to assert oneself, or ascribing too much value to something we like. However, if we find a healthy person who is able to make definitive choices that avoid the tendency toward self-sacrifice and lead to happiness, we'll find that the choices are often interlaced with the wonderful word, *No*.

"No, you cannot live with us."
"No, I will not give you a thin dime."
"No, you cannot borrow my car."
"No, you will not sing at my wedding."

Admittedly, the word *No* is a hard thing to say, especially the first time. After all, people have been trained from the beginning of time *not* to say it. We even laugh at that moment in a parent's life when a child first learns to say "No" . . . as if the word was in some way inappropriate. Granted, it should be used with wisdom, but there is value in saying "No," and when you finally garner the courage to try it, the rewards are great.

By deciding to say this simple word and then standing firmly by your decision, you have broken the chains of self-sacrifice and are guaranteed to live a life of contentment that will let you enjoy every glorious day to the fullest. Life is not a matter of getting or acquiring, but rather of avoiding and preventing. We start living the day we learn to say "No."

The Positive Thinking Deception

> How did Positive Thinking come to be synonymous with success? How could it promise so much, yet deliver so little?

It is important to remember that the reason we were all taught to avoid the word No as children was because we were using it to be disobedient. I whole-heartedly agree that children should be obedient—I'm just disappointed that the result is generations of adults who can't (okay, *won't*) take responsibility for their own happiness. For the next few chapters I want to tell you about some of the things that keep us from saying the word "No" as adults—and I'm going to start with a business mentality that I absolutely hate—*Positive Thinking*. This infamous dogma (about which many books have been written) was ostensibly developed to make the business environment better. But what it has actually done is provide a means for incompetent people to rule like tyrants over bright and creative workers.

To help you understand how well ensconced the dogma of Positive Thinking is, I'd like to tell you about a book I wrote in 1976 entitled, *How to Cure Yourself of Positive Thinking*. It was prompted by my strong dislike for the dogma and how it has been influencing people who should have known better for years.

The book sold reasonably well . . . but I received a lot of hate mail from people who apparently equated Positive Thinking with the faith and hope espoused by Christianity (keep in mind that Positive Thinking started as a business paradigm). Now, I'm all for hope and faith, but when Christians across the country accused me of being some sort of anti-Christian devil worshiper and demonstrated their *piety* by calling me obscene names in their anonymous letters, I took it a bit personally.

Those hate-mail-sending Christians seemed to have missed my chief objections to the overly simplistic Positive Thinking philosophy, which were—and still are—as follows:

1. When used as a tool of leadership, it is often manipulative: hurting subordinates, productivity, and the quality of work.

2. When used as a tool for self–help, it is often ineffectual and deceptive, robbing people of responsibility and hurting the very people it is meant to benefit.

Let me explain a bit more about my objections and show you how a simple *No* would be a much, much better solution.

A Manipulative Tool of Leadership

The Positive Thinking dogma is frequently used to force intelligent subordinates to accept management's bad ideas. Think about it. The superior–subordinate relationship can be reinforced quite respectably by a call for "a good, positive attitude." A *positive attitude* is much different than the Positive Thinking dogma because it respects the fact that superiors and subordinates alike can have good ideas and can contribute equally to the whole through hard work, mutual respect, and creativity. Contrast this with the Positive Thinking dogma, which teaches that a bad idea can bear fruit if we only think good thoughts about it—which is nothing more than ordering an intelligent person to support a bad idea. Remarkably, a well-placed *No* in such a situation has the potential to save money and (in the case of poorly conceived and designed products) even lives (assuming, of course, that management can deal with hearing the word in the first place).

I am reminded of my days in aerospace when I worked as a publications supervisor overseeing the work of technical editors, production people, and typists. We published reports and proposals on rigid deadlines. My job was to get ink on paper, coordinate with printers, and get the work out the door on schedule.

The rub came with the big proposals that came our way occasionally, projects that caught the eye of top management. Management operated with the fixed idea that only a person with a "technical background" could handle these proposals. (My degree is in English.) As a result, I was temporarily placed under the control of a person whose expertise was in the design of swept wings or supersonic nose cones, and this newly hatched publications *genius* was supposed to tell my experienced crew "how to get the job done." Management was apparently unaware that expertise in one field does not translate into an unrelated endeavor. These are people who would have hired Albert Einstein to coach an NFL team, or Robert Oppenheimer to conduct a symphony orchestra.

My task in this situation was to hold the monster at bay . . . lie and cheat . . . and make sure my people followed standard publication procedures while smiling obediently and pretending to comply with the inept manager's absurd instructions.

This was the art of saying "No" at its peak, although of necessity, it was an inaudible *No*. By working around this jerk (and his small army of subordinate jerks), we were able to meet deadlines and thereby save the company an inestimable sum of money. The great irony of all this is that the man who made this chicanery necessary was ultimately given a commendation by a smiling vice president. (Upon reflection, I think Oppenheimer might well have conducted the aforementioned orchestra—providing the musicians ignored him completely.)

◆ ◆ ◆

The reason the Positive Thinking dogma is loved by management and the business world in general is because it's based on the generally accepted but mistaken belief that something *positive* always resides on a higher ethical plane than something *negative* (which is another way of saying, "all good things must come from above"). For example, it is common for management to tell its employees that they have done "good work." But if the work was done for a bad cause, how "good" can it be? "Good work" per se can be done by anyone, from a highly educated college professor to a sniveling sycophant guarding some crime boss' illegal field of marijuana. Neither position nor profession makes any difference.

The Positive Thinking process takes outrageous advantage of this dichotomy by equating "good work" with the results of simply following a manager's plan. Indeed, in the business world the person who says "No" to a proposed plan of action—no matter how ill-conceived and patently dumb the plan may be—is labeled as being *Negative*. And if you become "too negative," you risk losing your job—which is an effective way of keeping subordinates in line (although often at the expense of creativity, productivity, and the quality of the employee's work). It may take more effort to allow workers to say "No" to a proposed plan of action, but the results are well worth the effort.

An Ineffectual and Deceptive Tool for Self-Help

The concept of Positive Thinking rarely works because it teaches the absurdity that merely thinking lovely, positive thoughts will somehow ensure success. In most cases, this aspect of Positive Thinking takes the form of expecting a particular result from a given desire, without working to ensure that result; this isn't especially dangerous, but it can lead to lost time and dashed hopes.

The real problem occurs when Positive Thinking is offered as a solution to people who genuinely need help, but haven't the resources to change their lives. This includes people who need training for a better job or counseling to save their marriage. In this case, Positive Thinking is about as effective as a rain dance during a drought. Thinking good thoughts will <u>NOT</u> make something

It's OK to Say No!

happen, and it is only a little short of cruel to tell someone that it will. From the point of view of helping people help themselves, the principle of Positive Thinking fails in two ways: first, it fails people when used as a means of self-defense against a world in which they don't always have control; second, it fails people by robbing them of responsibility. (This is perhaps the opinion my anonymous Christians hated so much.) Positive Thinking teaches that if we believe strongly enough that we can get a nice boat, the nice boat will come to us without our having to work for it. This is like saying, when the Lord blessed Isaac's flocks to multiply them, Isaac no longer needed to feed them or treat them for disease or protect them against predators or thieves—he simply needed to believe the miracle would happen—which, of course, wasn't true.

Positive Thinking used as Self-defense

The Positive Thinking philosophy assumes we have a degree of control over our lives that doesn't really exist. Much of what happens to us is decided by people sitting in executive conference rooms in distant cities. Take job security, for example. Almost every working man and woman has experienced a layoff—or at least worried about involuntary unemployment from the great axe of the "personnel cutback"—a cold, highly impersonal act that is generally brought about by forces and people unknown to those it affects. *Positive Thinking isn't going to save your job* —neither will incantations, candles, incense, nor animal sacrifice. And while assistance from the Divine may intervene to help, it is not going to occur simply because of Positive Thinking. We should all remember the adage, *pray as if everything depends on God, then work as if everything depends on you*. Positive Thinking combined with a good work ethic results in a *positive attitude*. Positive Thinking without a good work ethic is meaningless, if not self-destructive.

It is a fact that some of the most important things affecting our lives are completely beyond our sphere of influence: mortgage rates, loan decisions, petroleum prices, medical test results, insurance policy cancellations (even winning lottery numbers). And even in situations that we can control, performance counts much more than attitude. A good example is my California adult teaching credential. I had been teaching management courses for several years in private industry when I discovered that I could teach in the public school system if I acquired a state credential. To do this, I had to undergo two, three-unit courses which took place in all-day Saturday sessions for twelve weeks—a dozen consecutive Saturdays out of the life of a working man who values a free Saturday about as much as anyone can value anything.

I wasn't even halfway through the first session when I realized that the whole thing was going to be a waste of time and was valuable only as a means to an end. The class participants were required to sit in a large circle and "share" their experiences: something of a grown-up show-and-tell. Sometimes we acted out little playlets dealing with various teaching situations. Since my classmates would be teaching such diverse courses as auto-brake repair, dog grooming, oriental cooking, wood carving, and in my case, English and writing, the playlets had no applicability whatsoever and served little purpose other than to fill the long Saturday afternoons.

So here we come to the very soul of Positive Thinking. I could have attended these interminable sessions (over which I had no control) with a smile, full of enthusiasm and a firm belief that I would be a better teacher for attending, or I could endure them (as I did) as an ordeal I had to suffer through to get my credential. For those who contend that Positive Thinking would have helped me do better in the course, I can report that I received an "A"— primarily because I knew what kind of drivel they expected and gave it to them. (I used the word *share* a lot.)

I cite this example only to demonstrate that the Positive Thinking dogma has little to do with accomplishment. No matter how good your thoughts are, *if you don't produce, you don't prosper.* A mature person knows what must be done to get where he or she wants to be—which in my case was to surrender twelve precious Saturdays to be able to teach in the public school system. Neither I nor the other attendees gained anything from the classes, and none of us became better teachers for the experience. In this regard, the Positive Thinking mentality of the course (all the sharing and other like activities) failed to improve our skills.

Positive Thinking Robs Us of Responsibility

Possibly the worst effect the Positive Thinking mentality has on people is to cause them to relinquish responsibility. Positive Thinking becomes a way of life for people who don't want to run the risk of overtaxing their thought processes. It replaces the necessity for logical thought, the need for opposition to poorly conceived norms, and the benefit of formal education with the belief that if you just think positive enough thoughts, all the blessings these things bring will be yours. Why read Plato, Aquinas, Locke, Hegel, Kant, and Dewey when all one really needs to do is rub the magic lamp of Positive Thinking to get everything one wants out of life? Why study, why read, why expand one's knowledge? Why, with Positive Thinking, one doesn't have to dig, to compare, to analyze, or to question—only to accept the concepts of others as eternal truths and put all mental energies at rest.

Contrary to popular opinion, skepticism is not a bad thing. In fact, in an atmosphere where bad ideas abound, such as the applied sycophancy of private industry and the self-entrenching battlefront of the public sector, skepticism can be a vital factor in keeping the ship afloat. Often, the greatest thing you can accomplish in a given day is to kill a bad idea with a resounding "NO" (with the second greatest being to wound it severely by disregarding it and sending it off into the bushes). In fact, people who are willing to say "No" often provide the greatest benefit to mankind by spurring others into action. The greatest men and women in history did not achieve their status in life by thinking all day about how good life would be if only their dreams would come true. They achieved greatness through the hard work required to satisfy the skeptics—those people who initially rejected what they considered to be half-baked ideas—and eventually those "half-baked" ideas bore tremendous fruit.

Positive Thinking is not the business of the scholar, the semi-scholar, or the awakening intellect. Such individuals are geared more to reason and the assimilation of pragmatic facts. For them (and for me), the concept of a good attitude has been perverted into the frequently abused idea that we should blindly follow our leaders, never say "No," and smile while we do it!

. . . And if I can convince you of the fallacy of this perversion, I will have slain my own dragon.

Problem Perennials
(Responsibility vs. Obligation)

> True friendship is never based on need. A real friend is someone who doesn't want—or expect—anything from you.

In my opinion, people who talk about the value of sharing problems have little grounding in the realities of life. It isn't that I disapprove of people finding help when they need it. Everybody needs a shoulder to cry on from time to time to help them past the difficulties of life. Ideally, I tell you about a problem I can't resolve, and you help me figure out how to solve it. I grow from your help and don't need to bother you again the next time I face the same problem. In fact, I'm now in a position to help someone else. Eventually, everybody knows how to solve that particular problem and it no longer plagues mankind. Unfortunately, it usually doesn't work this way.

The truth is, precious little problem "sharing" goes on in the world. The reason for this is that many people believe it's the *problem* that's being shared when in fact, the thing that's being shared is the *solution*. As a result, there are problem *dumpers* (people who aren't looking for solutions but only want to unload on anyone who lacks the dexterity to get away from them) and the problem *dumpees* (people who consistently listen to other people's problems, but rarely have the opportunity to unload their own problems). Indeed, the problem dumpers tend to be *Problem Perennials*—people who *always* have a problem and *always* want to involve someone else in it—and any amount of joy they might bring into our lives is usually swamped by their unbearable demands.

This brings us to the second reason we don't say "No" to people. Since the middle ages society has taught people to have an inherent sense of *noblesse oblige* (the obligation of nobility, a/k/a the moral obligation to sacrifice ourselves for a cause). We're taught to feel an obligation toward people in need—and the problem dumpers take advantage of this. This isn't to say we shouldn't help people in need, I'm simply pointing out that we shouldn't feel obligated to help people who don't need or deserve our help. We're not responsible for the Problem Perennials who enter our lives.

Unfortunately, the odds are that we all know at least one person who is a Problem Perennial. Problem Perennials usually want something, which is why they lean on our sense of obligation (usually because they can't manage their lives by themselves), requiring us to be the responsible party. This makes them moochers—people who need a ride, a small loan, or a place to stay. Or maybe they want to borrow your camera, your typewriter, or your vacuum cleaner. Problem Perennials are usually one short step ahead of bill collectors and lawyers: they drive with a suspended license, owe everyone in town, and can't keep a job; but their current problem is always somebody else's fault.

"The bank mixed up my account."

"The police report was in error."

"The boss blamed the wrong person."

"The witness was lying."

Isn't it odd that these problems rarely seem to plague the rest of us?

Characteristics of the Problem Perennial

You're not doing a Problem Perennial a favor by being responsible for them, nor are you helping them by caving in to your sense of obligation. Where helping the deserving needy brings joy because your help changes their lives, helping Problem Perennials changes nothing and only guarantees they'll be back for more. This behavior makes them prime candidates for an emphatic, "No!"

There are several distinguishing characteristics that bind all Problem Perennials into one big, undesirable lump, and knowing what these characteristics are will help us to say "No" when they lean on us.

1. _They never learn_. This characteristic is truly constant. There are Problem Perennials still unborn who will buy lightning-rod franchises or swampland in Florida. The poor soul who makes stupid investments and loses his shirt at age 25 will be surrendering the same shirt at age 70—still trying for that big score. It shouldn't surprise you to discover that Problem Perennials tend to be the biggest advocates of Positive Thinking—it's usually the only way they can get people to agree with them.

Consider the plight of a female Problem Perennial who is married to a husband who comes home drunk every night and beats her. She will eventually divorce him, then marry a man who— guess what?—comes home drunk every night and beats her.

Or consider the hypochondriac who receives neither attention nor sympathy for his fancied illnesses but who will continue indefinitely with the ailment routine, each time gaining nothing from it.

Problem Perennials are almost always repeaters, and they learn absolutely nothing from experiences that should be sufficient to deter even preschoolers from making mistakes.

2. _They need to tell their story—again and again and again_. Problem Perennials always have the need to air their problems, and no matter what course a conversation takes, they're going to do it. A discussion on grain subsidies, for example, might bring out the following response: "George and I were discussing that very subject the day before he ran off with that tramp and left me

with three children to raise." Or, "That no good lying boss of mine used to write letters to the paper about grain subsidies. He fired me because he knew that I had the goods on him." Or the ever popular, "I have a good book on that subject, but I've been too sick to read it . . . ."

A Problem Perennial can steer a conversation in his or her direction no matter what the original topic, whether it be nuclear disarmament, euthanasia, animal experimentation, or the relative advantages and disadvantages of term life insurance. A real professional can even sense a drift in the topic and flawlessly steer the conversation right back to the "fleeing husband" or the "vengeful employer." It's a morbidly fascinating and utterly reprehensible talent.

3. *They always need something from you.* If someone is going to hit you up for money (or anything else), they will go along with sports, politics, or what-good-books-have-you-read-lately for just so long, then comes the bite. This is the primary reason that nobody wants these people around: they can't walk away without getting *something* from you. Problem Perennials don't care one iota if you can't afford to give them money or if it is going to be an inconvenience for you to drive them someplace. They don't care if you have to miss a day of work to tend to their needs or if you don't want them driving your car. These telephone marathoners don't care in the least that their victims might have something else to do. I find it amazing that people with a long history of marital problems have no interest in learning that other people may have marital problems, too.

Simply put, Problem Perennials don't want to hear about other people's problems and don't care about other people's needs—they only care about (and want to talk about) their own. *They are oblivious to other people's needs.*

4. *They're driven to bring other people into their misery.* Problem Perennials are vitally concerned with one-way sharing. Whatever

the problem, anyone within a five-mile radius must be a part of it. Here we see the drunk who cannot drink alone, or the neglected spouse who wants to harangue the world with an endless monologue. Nor can we overlook that bundle of cheer who is still telling her grown children about the agonies of childbirth and how she suffered bringing them into the world. (And these people wonder why they aren't invited anywhere?)

You can always identify a Problem Perennial by the fact that *everybody* knows who they are, knows what their complaints are, and has a desire to avoid them.

5. *They can tune any subject into the "problem channel."* Problem Perennials who have come to air their problems are going to do it, no matter what. *They are unscrupulous.* Every one of them comes equipped with a lever, often a blood relationship or some other personal bond, which they use to exploit family, friends, old school ties, and presumably even God and the flag. This is what I meant when I said that Problem Perennials know we all have a sense of obligation which they can use to their advantage. These people will use every known ploy to make you act in their behalf. The defense to this exploitation is to remain firm and say "No" to their appeals. Any sign of weakening will bring on a full attack, and the slightest rift often leads to total collapse. These people are cagey foes indeed, and they know how to make it past the moat and into your castle.

6. *They don't want their problems solved.* Without doubt, the most significant characteristic that distinguishes Problem Perennials is that they have learned to treasure their problems like collections of fine Dresden china or Hummel figurines. They love their problems, but above all, they *need* them. Problems are their only link with mankind. The Problem Perennial sees complaining as communication: to talk is to gripe. Problems are their world, so don't talk to them about solutions. They don't want to hear them.

✦ ✦ ✦

Remember, we are *not* talking about people with normal—and therefore solvable—problems. We are discussing people with chronic problems, usually self-inflicted, that will never go away. These people are determined to keep the pot boiling, and they rely on your sense of obligation to do so. And there is no defense against them except the word *NO*.

Ploys of the Problem Perennial

It is worth taking time to describe the various ploys used by Problem Perennials to leverage our sense of obligation and gain access to our lives. After all, nothing annoys an honest person more than knowing they've been *used,* so knowing how Problem Perennials lay their traps is the first step in avoiding them.

Exploitation: A lot of the stress a Problem Perennial can bring to bear can be attributed directly to the "relationship" lever that he or she exploits to work on our emotions and make us act in an illogical manner. For example, a case of the "old-town tie" occurred a few years ago with a friend of mine named Nora. Nora received a phone call one morning from a woman named Daphne, whom Nora had known slightly during her high school years in Minnesota. Daphne, a single woman in her forties, had just arrived in town . . . had in fact moved there . . . and wanted to "get together." Nora invited her over. They spent a few pleasant hours reminiscing about mutual friends and Daphne stayed for dinner. She was also back the next night, and at least three nights a week from that point on. When Nora and her husband Bill went out to dinner, Daphne went along, and when they stayed home, Daphne was there, too. They had clearly become a threesome.

When Bill complained that he had had about enough of Daphne, the explanation was always, "Be patient. She's new in town and doesn't know anyone." Can you see how Daphne had taken advantage of Nora's sense of obligation toward a friend?

After a year, however, it became readily apparent that Daphne had no interest in meeting anyone or in getting a life of her own. Her problem was (and always would be) that she didn't know anyone, but as long as she had Nora and Bill, she wouldn't even make the effort. She would never solve her problem because she didn't want it solved. The "old friendship" was fictionalized to the point that she and Nora were inseparable as teenagers, when the truth was, they had hardly known each other.

By this time Nora had clearly reached the end of her rope, but she had no idea how to handle the situation. Bill stepped in and settled it for her. He told Daphne to back off and give them some space, and to find a life of her own that didn't involve them. In short, he said, "No!" to her unwelcome intrusions.

Daphne, incensed, quit her job and moved back to Minnesota, firmly believing that Bill had maliciously broken up an old friendship. Of course, this was not true, but there is one thing he did accomplish—he got Daphne off their backs forever.

Pressure: Another ploy of the Perennials is to back their marks into a corner and attempt to leave them no way out. For instance, "I have to come up with $714.18 by midnight or my family will be put out onto the street and I will be marched to the stockade and trampled to death by wild horses." Well, if the half-wit could see this coming, why didn't he look for advice a long time ago?

This is a common scenario with Perennials. They never recognize their weaknesses and therefore, don't look for advice to prevent their inevitable catastrophes. Instead, they mismanage right down the line, tell no one, then expect a bailout from someone else once they've run out of options. (Watch out for their stories. They usually contain a grain of truth, but they'll pad the facts to make sure you're cozy in that corner and feel very responsible for their future.)

If I could ever instill a single attitude into anyone, it would be a profound resentment at being backed into a corner and then (seemingly) given no choice but to respond as directed. Here's a more subtle example, "If I don't find the money in the next few days, the bank will take my car. Don't you have equity in your house you can use to help me?" For my part, I would refuse on the sole grounds of resentment, because anyone who would presume that I could be so misused and manipulated deserves no consideration whatsoever.

If, however, you need a more compassionate reason than this for saying "No," then consider compassion for yourself! After all, you're not filing bankruptcy, it isn't your car at stake, you've acted responsibly—and you darn well want to keep it that way. Where was this person months before when a simple change in lifestyle could have solved his problem? You didn't make any financial mistakes, so why should you pay for the mistakes of the Problem Perennial?

Remember, I'm not advocating that you throw every needy person out into the street—I'm talking about not letting yourself become the quick-fix for people who should have known better. You are responsible for yourself and the well-being of your family (to a point—we'll get to that shortly), but you are in no way obligated to fix problems in the lives of people who, through their own negligence, regularly have them.

Guilt: Let us remember—and never forget—that Problem Perennials thrive on other people's guilt. They cannot exist without it. They have to convince the rest of us that "less fortunate" includes those people who blew their rent money at the race track, or snorted it up their noses, or who bought things they couldn't afford and are now facing payback time. However, the person who refuses to work or to manage his or her life in even the simplest way is _not_ "less fortunate." People who bring on their own misfortunes (usually after repeated warnings) are not to be pitied and are undeserving of anyone's compassion. There are too many deserving and legitimately needy people in the world for anyone to be wasting time and money on those who repeatedly bring the world down upon their own heads.

This reminds me of another sad story involving some very nice people—Chuck and Peggy. They lived on a cul-de-sac in Los Angeles that was filled with starter homes for young couples who hoped to move on to better things. Chuck, an aeronautical engineer, was making a better than average salary and had prospects of living a long and comfortable life. Peggy worked as a technical writer and also earned a reasonably good salary. Like most young couples, they looked forward to children, a better house, and maybe seeing Paris before they died. The only flaw in this plan was Peggy's brother Larry, a lifelong Problem Perennial whose sole function in life seemed to be showing up at Chuck and Peggy's doorstep several times a year and mooching money, favors, and ". . . a place to stay until I can get back on my feet."

Chuck eventually grew tired of this constant albatross around his neck and told Larry, "*No,*" which Peggy resented. As she said, "He *is* my brother." She kept sending him money, but without telling Chuck. Eventually—and inevitably—Chuck found out. They argued and ultimately divorced, with Larry being the sole cause.

Today, more than 25 years later, Chuck is remarried (his wife is an only child, incidentally) and Peggy lives alone in Los Angeles. She still gives regular handouts to Larry ("After all, he *is* my brother") and looks forward to the day when Larry will get back on his feet and start catching a few of those good breaks that seem to go to everyone else.

Peggy is the personification of the professional mark. Larry has known all his life that there will always be "something in the well"—a financial handout, a meal, a place to stay, and someone to lie for him and not condemn him for being the loathsome parasite that he is. Peggy benefits by escaping guilt, and this is exactly the way Larry wants it. The more guilt that Peggy feels, the better it is for him. (The only big winner is Chuck, who is out of the whole mess forever.)

Another family story I've come across that has a happier ending involves Andy, who also had a brush with a Problem Perennial. Andy is now an architect in Seattle, but his story starts in Los

Angeles at a time when he had been divorced for about five years. When he met Marcy, a photographer and an attractive, personable young woman, it seemed obvious that they were a perfect match. In fact, they became engaged when they had known each other for only a few months.

There was a strange piece to the puzzle, however. Marcy was never able to be with Andy on Sundays, and after some intense questioning, Andy learned that she, her two brothers, and her brothers' wives were expected to be at "Daddy's" graveside every Sunday. This Sunday gathering of the clan was a regular event. Mother demanded it, and no excuses were accepted. The woman could not let go. Therefore, no one else was allowed to let go either, and the entire family went as a sop to the mother's hang-up. When Marcy's mother expressed grief she expected a cheering section. For Marcy, it was a 60-mile drive each way, but she hadn't missed a Sunday in the seven years since her father had shuffled off this mortal coil.

When all of this business finally came out into the open, Marcy went a step further. She told Andy that he would be expected to participate after they were married. This rang an immediate bell in Andy's head: no Sunday golf, no weekend trips, and no goofing off around the apartment pool. Even more, he resented the fact that it was *expected*. Andy thought about it for all of 15 seconds and told Marcy that he was not about to spend his Sundays sitting in a cemetery. They argued and broke up, but eventually got back together when Marcy shrugged off the guilt of saying "*No*" to her mother and realized what it meant to be an adult. She told her mother that she would no longer be part of her Sunday sickness, and she has never regretted it. She and Andy have been married for over eight years now, and Mother (so far as I know) has survived this mutiny in her ranks.

Inability to Compromise: Problem Perennials have probably ruined more lives than all of the dictators, racketeers, terrorists, and serial killers combined. These people live by keeping everyone else in line, and there is no way to reason with them. They don't want to give an inch because they can't. They don't believe in compromise because it puts them out of business. Their entire existence is based on their problems taking precedence over all other things. When this is challenged, they lose. Theirs is a risky business, but to them, the fight is worth it. Losing means total, crushing defeat and (even worse) the possibility that they might have to start living (and even thinking) like responsible human beings. For them, this won't do at all.

Trying to reach an accommodation with Problem Perennials has been about as successful as man's eternal battle against cockroaches and gophers (a battle man is *not* winning). There are only two courses of action available when dealing with these people: we can play it their way and spend a lifetime both supporting them and listening to an eternal monologue about how society has "done them wrong," or we can say "*No,*" and walk away happy.

Your Relationship to the Problem Perennial

Let me wrap up this discussion of the Problem Perennial by reminding you that there are reasonable limits to our responsibilities and our obligations. These limits are important when working out our relationship with Problem Perennials.

Understanding and caring

We hear a lot about *understanding* these days and modern *noblesse oblige* teaches that we should first understand the problems of our fellow beings, then act in their behalf. Taken to the extremes of today's liberals, this is a supposition that no sane person could ever justify. Social dogooders would have us believe that if we could just *understand people*, we would want to help them (i.e., give money to someone who is going to flush it down the sewer, or spend an evening being ground into the floor by a repetitive account of someone's self-made problems). Thus, we are left with the conclusion that we must listen to these people, and that if we listen to them, we are *obligated* to help them. (But who listens to the listeners? Most assuredly not the Problem Perennials.)

When used in this manner, understanding will be interpreted by the Problem Perennial as *approval,* which isn't the case at all. So let's dispense with that notion now and forever: *understanding has nothing to do with approval.*

For example, people during World War II certainly understood Adolf Hitler. And there was no lack of understanding for Judas Iscariot, Jack the Ripper, Al Capone, and the Freeway Strangler. These people were understood completely, but no one in their right mind would *approve* of their actions.

When used correctly, understanding truly leads to caring (which includes caring for yourself). If you understand what type of people Problem Perennials are, what drives them, and how they try to use you, you will do the very best thing for both them and you: you'll tell them in no uncertain terms, "No!"

Priorities

An important factor to consider when dealing with Problem Perennials is the inevitable hardship that your family will suffer if, for example, you plunge deeper into debt. Why should your spouse and children suffer from an added financial burden while the Problem Perennial escapes justice in Pago Pago or the Australian Outback? The answer, clearly, is that none of you should pay the price. Put your priorities in order and let this disgusting individual eat prison food for awhile.

Morality is a cloudy thing indeed, and we often find ourselves groping for the *right* thing to do. Too often we grope in the wrong direction and make holy hash out of virtue. When we talk about helping our fellowman—or *caring,* as the popular notion is expressed—we often take as a blanket moral dictum the belief that we must help anyone and everyone who is in trouble, even if innocent people get hurt. This, of course, is absolute rubbish.

It is our privilege to help those people who deserve our help whenever we are capable of doing so, but the Problem Perennials do not fall into this category. And they certainly are not responsible enough to judge their own worthiness (it isn't even reasonable to expect them to do so)—we have to make that judgment. Even if we should decide that a person is worthy of our assistance, we must then determine if such help will impose a hardship on others (especially our immediate family). Thanks, however, to our inbred sense of responsibility, saying "*No*" often brings about feelings of guilt. This is why understanding our priorities is so important: you first, your family second, your immediate relatives third (at best), and everybody else *last*.

And for those of you who think the "me first" is selfish, remember that if you can't help yourself, you're in no position to help another.

Responsibility and Obligation

This is where it all starts coming together. When a Problem Perennial stands on your doorstep with a heart-wrenching story and a hand halfway into your wallet, ask yourself the following questions: are you responsible for this person's welfare? Is there any reason that you are morally bound to keep this person afloat? If the answer is *No*, then have you signed any papers or even agreed with a handshake that you will be on hand to alleviate this person's problems? If the answer is still *No*, then you have scored a double "Noway" and you are free of the situation completely.

All of this leads to the heart of what we really owe the people who make demands on us. Put succinctly, *those who didn't cause a mess are not responsible to clean it up!*

✦ ✦ ✦

Responsibility is an accountability, usually moral, for behaving in a certain way. We are responsible for the welfare and happiness of our spouses, our children, and to a lesser extent, our elderly parents. We also have a responsibility to be good neighbors and good citizens. We are <u>not</u> responsible for the actions of our grown children, distant cousins, the guy across the street, or old Little League teammates.

An obligation is a somewhat different thing. Here we are talking about a binding promise, a good example being a formal debt. When we borrow money, we sign a paper agreeing to the terms of the loan and are obligated to repay it. Employment is also largely a matter of obligation. On accepting a job, we agree to work certain hours at a specified salary and to perform in a manner consistent with the standards of the workplace.

Mature individuals understand the difference between responsibilities and obligations, as well as those things that are *not* responsibilities or obligations, and will not accept a debt (financial or otherwise) that clearly is not theirs. However, the Problem Perennial desperately wants you to believe otherwise.

It's Okay to Say No—Really!

We often make the mistake of believing that we can compromise our way to happiness. You give, I give, we meet somewhere in the middle, and everybody goes away happy. But this is a sunshine philosophy that tends to break down when we're faced with a Problem Perennial.

Remember that a Problem Perennial is someone with no other interest in life than his own *big* problem. He introduces the subject, won't get off the subject, and rejects all suggested solutions. These people aren't going to change, so the strategy of waiting them out and hoping for the best really isn't an option. *You* have to change things, distasteful as that might sound, and this is accomplished only by employing that wonderful word, "No." Once the deed is done, the world is immediately a better place.

An interesting thing about the word No is the great sense of relief that it brings us once it is spoken. The hours prior to this traumatic oral delivery can be stressful and taxing. Many people spend sleepless nights because the morning is going to bring about a confrontation with a Problem Perennial who has an impossible request. Yet, once the word is uttered, once it is out in the air, one wonders why all of the stress was necessary.

It is truly one of life's most rewarding moments when you muster the courage to say "No" to an undeserving Problem Perennial. The sun will shine on the Yellow Brick Road, the villagers will dance in the streets, the birds will sing, and the celestial chorus will join in a heaven-sent rendition of, "Happy Days Are Here Again."

Above all, you are free. The word No does this for people.

The Family

> Blood is NOT thicker than water.
> So when we speak of family ties, let
> us not forget the noose.

I have spoken with many people who either work or have worked in mental institutions. To date, I have yet to meet anyone who can report a patient who was put there because of the national debt, the atomic bomb, the rising divorce rate, or the depletion of the rain forests. The most common reason for residency in a mental institution is *family:* the stresses, strains, and fancied obligations of blood ties. We put our children, spouses, parents, and siblings into locked rooms by our constant and unyielding demands—which opens the door for the third reason we don't say "No": the errant belief that blood is thicker than water. (The third edition of the New Dictionary of Cultural Literacy defines the phrase "blood is thicker than water" to mean, "our loyalty to our family—that is, to our blood relations—is strong no matter how we may feel about them." It's a phrase the mafia lives and dies by and it singularly describes this remarkable triumph of emotion over the intellect: our ability to obligate ourselves unreasonably to our family.)

I remember speaking with a young lady while I was a guest on a radio talk show in Miami. The topic, of course, was the word No, and I felt that most of the people who called desperately needed some prodding in the No direction. The best example among the callers was a 31-year-old woman who had never had a date and rarely left her home at night. The reason? She *owed* it to her parents to stay home and tend to their needs. After all, they had given her life and looked after her during her childhood, so she felt she was in their debt. To make her bondage even more complete, she wasn't even allowed to keep her paycheck. Instead, she received an allowance for lunch and small purchases. It had come to this point only because it was a lifetime pattern that she didn't know how to change. Fortunately, she had summoned the courage to call the radio program I was on and hear a sympathetic man (me) tell her to get out of that house immediately. (In fact, I even offered to help her pack.)

Let me tell you about a similar turn-over-your-check situation that I listened to on Toni Grant's radio talk show in Los Angeles sometime in the 1980's. It involved a milksop who went to work every day of his life without a penny in his pocket. His loving wife saw no need for him to have any money because he had a gasoline credit card and his company had a cafeteria arrangement whereby the cost of the lunch was deducted from the employee's paycheck. The loving wife (naturally) checked the take-home pay and the gasoline bill carefully to assure that no funny business was going on. (It is *obviously* a well-known fact that men with no money in their pockets really tear up the pea patch when they're away from their wives.)

Although these cases seem to be rather extreme, they really aren't that far away from the norm. Both are examples of strong family members keeping weaker members under their thumbs until the inevitable state of torpor takes over. In both of these cases, the answer is to *say "No,"* loudly and clearly. These aren't situations that need "talking over" or any "exchange of viewpoints." After all, what predator ever "talked it over" with his or her victim?

One does not reason with the unreasonable.

✦ ✦ ✦

It's OK to Say No!

I'm going to spend the rest of this chapter explaining to you how and why families can drain you physically, emotionally, and financially. Understand that I'm not talking about the normal love and care that should exist between family members. I'm talking about the evil people who take advantage of the idea that blood is thicker than water just to use you.

✦ ✦ ✦

Many people spend the better part of a lifetime hoping that a situation will change, but familial strangleholds are not self-correcting. When a person finds something that works—illness, obligation, or even simple brute strength—there will be no voluntary retreat. People simply do not give up something that works every time. (And keep in mind, *waiting for people to reform themselves is like standing on the wrong street and waiting for a bus that never comes.)*

Violence Begets Control

I have seen cases where something as simple as a nasty disposition has been used to keep other family members in line. Some people are so afraid of conflict they'll do anything to keep the "monster" placated. When a child learns that being nasty and abusive gets results, he grows into adulthood with that particular hand tool hooked to his belt; if it got him out of helping with the dishes or pulling weeds at the age of eight, it will do wonders at 38.

Unfortunately for many of us, the personal threat of violence is a successful stratagem an oppressor can use to get his or her way. And more often than not, our reaction to this behavior is to do this person's work ourselves . . . or to hand over our money . . . or to turn over the car keys . . . or even to open the guest room door rather than fight about it. People with bad dispositions learn early on that bile (or, to use the modern psycho-phrase, *bullying*) pays off. They learn that people around them will give in rather than face abuse. So, they put this bile to work and reload for the next volley.

It seems rather incredible that these abusive people are so evenly spread among the families of America. An old friend of mine (whom we call the Sage of Bakersfield) once evolved a theory that the Almighty, as part of a grand plan, put one abuser, one moocher, and one hypochondriac into every family. My friend calls it the *Theory of Obnoxious Dispersion*. It's an interesting concept that looks credible on the surface—although it would take a considerable amount of research to establish its validity. Also, I'm not at all sure about the cause and effect. Maybe the family dynamic creates its own undesirable members. My own belief is that moochers and hypochondriacs are environmentally created, but nasty, abusive people are just born that way. Their personalities are determined at the moment of conception, and once they find that abuse pays off for them, they don't even bother with a cover-up; they just carry their behavior with them until the end, like having six toes.

The Ties That Bind

There are more subtle ways than the threat of violence for a family member to get his or her way. I often meet less-than-intrepid family members who have difficulty coming up for air when they're buried under layers of that hoary old bromide, *blood is thicker than water*. Blood ties (it would seem to any rational person) are for helping and caring, not for subjugating —and certainly not for paying back old debts. But if there is one phrase more responsible than any other for the break-up of the American family, it's "You owe me."

It all comes back to the concepts of obligation and responsibility discussed in the previous chapter. People who give birth have a responsibility to take care of their children until they are able to take care of themselves. There is no reciprocal responsibility, and obligation doesn't enter into it at all.

For example, if a son or daughter wants to look after an aging parent, it should be a

> Remember, you are responsible for your actions, but obligated by circumstance imposed upon you by external forces or by your decisions.

matter of simple love—there's no *balancing of the ledger* involved. This is not an accounting class. Even the Bible teaches that we should honor our father and our mother, but I don't interpret this to mean that we are obligated to them for the rest of our lives. We do not owe anything to anyone for being born and don't let yourself be told otherwise. Child-rearing does not warrant a curtain call; it's what you're supposed to do when you have children.

Do you remember in Chapter One when I said that one of the problems with Positive Thinking is that there are aspects of life outside our control, and that not all the happy optimism in the world will change their influence on our lives? In like manner, we clearly have no obligation to, or responsibility for, situations that we cannot control. If the family loser gets into one mess after another without our consent or knowledge, then we are neither obligated to bail him out nor responsible for his actions. For example, if Mom and Dad advise a daughter not to marry an obvious lout and she ignores that advice, why should they have the responsibility to take her back (often two children and twenty black eyes later)? It's one thing to argue that a person matures by making his own mistakes; it's another thing altogether when an innocent bystander has to pay for those mistakes.

It seems to me that far too often, responsible people are told to mind their own business. Then the day arrives when the family loser has to pay for his or her mistakes, and suddenly the accountability for those mistakes magically becomes the purview of the responsible party.

"You owe me," they claim.

I don't think so! Don't get me wrong. Strong family relationships are important, but too often the family is a festering breeding ground for the debt-and-obligation game. The only way to fight back is to take a long and serious look at what you *do* and *do not* owe someone. Certainly, you have no obligation to assume responsibility for a problem that is not of your own making, and there's no need to feel guilty about saying *"No"* in such a situation.

✦   ✦   ✦

It's OK to Say No!

"I'll Scratch Your Back If You'll Scratch Mine." (Now Scratch It Again . . . and Again . . . and Again . . .)

Let's not forget that *helping* someone does not necessarily incur an *obligation*. When a parent voluntarily helps a son or daughter make a down-payment on a house, or one brother helps another start a business, we're talking about voluntary gestures of goodwill. These are things that a person wants to do, and indeed feels good about doing—and they have nothing to do with obligation. A gift is an act of love, not part of the old you-owe-it-to-me game. An obligation, on the other hand, is more closely connected with the yoke and the whip. If you *want* to be obligated to someone, then write up a contract. In fact, nothing can save a family better than the habit of writing well-constructed contracts so that everybody knows exactly when an obligation ends. Let me give you an example:

One couple of our acquaintance, Art and Marilyn, once lived in Santa Monica. (People living in Florida and Southern California are especially vulnerable to family incursions because the locations are so desirable to vacationers.) They came from Wisconsin and both of them were from large families. The relatives were understandably thrilled to have a California connection. ("Geez, they're right at the beach!")

Art and Marilyn were good friends of ours, but we gave up seeing them between May and September. Why? Because they were always tied up with relatives. The Folks in Wisconsin would get together during the winter and map out their vacation plans. ("We'll take the last two weeks of May, Joe and Margaret get the first two weeks of June, and Sam and Edna will take the last two weeks of June. Okay, now for July . . . .")

When they came, they all expected the full Los Angeles treatment: Disneyland, Universal City, Dodger and Angel Stadiums, movie-stars' homes, and the customary overnighter in San Diego or Santa Barbara. This applied to *each* group; once one had gone, the next wave arrived and expected the same thing. Even though they paid their own way (they had been saving all year) Art and Marilyn had to pay for themselves, over and over and over again. They went into the fall season not only dead broke, but physically exhausted.

After five straight summers of this they decided that they had had enough. But how could they put a stop to it without (get ready) "hurting their relatives' feelings"? Our friends had long since passed the point of hoping for relief . . . a time when their family would decide that the California relations needed a rest—might even want a summer vacation of their own! Such wishing was, of course, an exercise in futility, because people who would swarm on a relative like a plague of locusts year after year would never of their own volition call a halt. They just keep coming, and coming, and coming. That's the way locusts move; a natural flow that doesn't reroute itself.

I had lunch with Art one day and he asked if I had any kind of solution (short of doing the one thing that had to be done). They had discussed going away for the summer, but they couldn't afford to stay anywhere long and he would need to take an unpaid leave of absence. They had also discussed turning the tables and going to Wisconsin, but this was only a temporary reprieve—the locusts would just follow them back.

The only answer—which neither one of them wanted to hear—was to write a letter putting a stop to it all. The problem had come down to the same bedrock where so many problems land. A person must either put up with a miserable situation, or make someone unhappy and end it. We can spend the rest of our lives looking for that third road to travel, but it's never going to be there.

Our friends finally bit the bullet and did what had to be done. They wrote the letter, made copious Xerox copies, and sent them to the entire distribution list in Wisconsin. They made their home available only for the first two weeks of June, and they suggested that family members draw lots for the visiting rights. The letter also stated that Art would not be taking his vacation at this time because he and Marilyn might like to take a vacation of their own.

Of course, this caused a great uproar with both families, and no one in Wisconsin was able to work up a grain of understanding for our friends' position. However, the deed was done. (Art retired a few years ago and moved Marilyn to Idaho . . . where no one ever visits them. There's a lot to be said for Idaho.)

Compromise Doesn't Always Work

In all of these cases, I have cited the difficulty that people have in saying "No" to anyone who might in any way be considered family. In every case, the alternative to saying "No" is to put up with an unpleasant or impossible situation. This is a fact that simply must be faced. We love our families, but that doesn't mean everything they do to us is *right*.

The problem arises from the same *noblesse oblige* I spoke about earlier, only this time the "obligation of nobility" refers to the idea that we should *play fair*—and we're taught that playing fair means compromising our position so that everything is equal (a/k/a, sacrifice ourselves).

This, of course, is impossible. Nothing is ever completely equal. Despite this, we are taught from birth to grave to rely on this Great Myth of Compromise. We are taught (and honestly believe, despite what our capitalist economy proves) that there is always a way to solve a problem by having both sides talk it over, give a little, and then meet somewhere in the middle. It is instilled in us as children, and we believe, *believe, BELIEVE,* even though it isn't true at all. Life teaches us that for the most part we do not reach agreements by compromise, but rather by one side giving in completely. This is the way the world works and it is demonstrated daily. For example:

- Children go to public school, private school, or are home schooled—they don't do a little of each at the same time.
- Someone's mother lives with them *or* does not live with them.

- I accept the transfer *or* I do not accept the transfer.
- We buy a new car this year *or* we do not buy a new car this year.
- We have dinner at home *or* we have dinner out.

Most of the decisions we make are *either/or* decisions, yet we start each day firmly believing that all problems can be discussed and resolved through compromise. The result is that we hit a brick wall and our beliefs are shattered—again. And we act surprised each time this happens, even though it happens almost every day. (For example, when was the last time you successfully worked out your differences with the political shark at your office?)

Family problems should always be filed under "E" for Either/ Or. They just don't lend themselves to compromise. There is no middle ground—unless you're willing to completely sacrifice your own happiness. But what kind of a compromise is that? I'm trying to teach you to *break* that habit. Each decision involving family comes down to a *Yes* or a *No* and with *No* being strongly discouraged from birth, therein lies the formula for instant stress.

The Causes of Family Stress

Family derived stress can be broken into five basic categories, which I call the *Five Stressful Expectations:*

1. The Presence Expectation
2. The Performance Expectation
3. The Acceptance Expectation
4. The Allegiance Expectation
5. The Accommodation Expectation

The <u>*Presence Expectation*</u> was illustrated in the previous chapter by the story of Andy and Marcy where Marcy's presence was expected every Sunday at the cemetery to accommodate her mother's need to relive her husband's death. It is also evident when one is expected for certain holidays or even Sunday dinner, regardless of your own personal wishes. At holiday time we often hear the sad stories of people who are alone, but we never hear of the people forced to go somewhere they don't want to be and to associate with people they don't particularly like. Such people might (and often do) *prefer* to be alone.

The <u>*Performance Expectation*</u> does its damage with people who are expected to achieve certain standards when they lack either the ability or the interest to attain them. For example, Mother and Dad have college degrees, so their children are expected to earn degrees, which is a reasonable expectation of any young person with the ability to make it through college. Suppose, however, that one of their children is not a student and had great difficulty making it through high school. This one doesn't have a prayer of getting through the freshman year at Mortimer Snerd Community College. He or she will fail to meet this expectation and therefore disappoint the parents, grandparents, aunts, uncles, cousins, and presumably even the family next door.

I know of a specific case in which a young man obtained a master's degree, with academic honors, then accepted a job as a letter carrier. Why? Because he knew that he would be happy doing that for a living (and in fact, he was). His mother and wife joined forces in a continuing harangue, however, about "amounting to something," which in his case meant doing something that he hated. This seems to be a uniquely American belief: anyone who isn't living up to his potential (which usually means doing something that he hates) really isn't trying. In this "Case of the Happy Letter Carrier," there seemed to be no consideration of the fact that he was a thoroughly happy man making a descent living. Instead, the two most important women in his life felt his unused college degree was the only credible career path. In their minds, this man had somehow failed them, the rest of the family, and even the entire North American continent when the truth was, he hadn't failed *anyone*. It is unfortunate that so few people understand the idea of obtaining a degree solely to become an educated person, and not to find a place in some corporate hierarchy.

The *Acceptance Expectation* concerns itself with accepting set family beliefs. Let's say that the family—aunts, uncles, nephews, nieces, in fact the whole clan—draws names from a hat each year to determine who gives a gift to whom for Christmas. But one of the family members doesn't like the person whose name he drew and doesn't want to participate. Or, even worse, what if the whole family is Roman Catholic and one of the kids decides to become a Mormon? Families can become absolutely bent out of shape when they confront something they consider unacceptable to the family norm. What about the person who doesn't want to participate in a family activity? Or what about the person who doesn't vote the same way the family votes, or think the way the family thinks on any given issue? The person who doesn't want to play softball in the park on Sunday (or even *be* in the park on Sunday) certainly isn't depriving anyone else of the experience. Some families would respect this person's right to make an individual decision, but many do not.

Here's an example of the hot water you can get into when you marry into another family that has Acceptance Expectations. Many years ago, I worked with a young man who married a secretary in our department. As I later learned, she was the youngest and the only girl in a family of five children. These people were avid hunters, and she was taken along on their hunting trips from the time she could barely walk. She had no memory of anything but Dad and her brothers declaring war on every four-footed creature in the forest.

Shortly after their wedding, the bride's Dad and her brothers gave the new husband a rifle, an expensive hunting outfit, and complete instructions on the correct way to blow a deer's tiny brains into the Great Beyond. They also informed the groom that he would be expected to join them in the woods from that moment on. To marry into that family was to be an instant deer slayer.

At that precise moment, this young man was presented with a major problem. He had known that these people were hunters, but he hadn't any idea that he was to be included in their carnal revelry. He also saw no reason to march off into the woods and shoot an animal, nor did he have the slightest desire to sleep on the ground or to hunker down by a fire on a cold autumn night (his idea of a vacation was a room with a view in San Francisco.) He told this to the family and said that he hoped they could get their money back on the hunting equipment.

Now, up to this point you probably thought this was a better example of the *Presence Expectation*—and indeed, it would be—if it were not for what happened next. The new husband's attempt to say "No" to a practice he wanted no part of immediately sparked great resentment and he became an instant outsider. *The interpretation of his refusal to hunt was that he was condemning them and, by so doing, setting himself "above" his wife's family.* It was taken as an insult when the truth was, he had said nothing more than that he didn't want to go hunting. His wife took the family's side and the friction only increased. She joined in the collective booing and hissing and they were divorced within a year. That's an awfully high price to pay for a family's anal desire to have a new family member conform to their beliefs—after all, the guy simply didn't want to hunt.

The *Allegiance Expectation* probably hits harder than any of the other expectations. This one puts blood relationships above the law—even above accepted standards of morality and decency. Those who believe in the Allegiance Expectation would expect one family member to hide another if that person were escaping from the law, or to help conceal a transgression even when they knew that the person was guilty.

I recall a case that I encountered many years ago when I was in college. Gordon, a classmate of mine, was an excellent student. He graduated with high honors, which he earned through hard work and by giving up many of the good times that are usually associated with college life. Gordon had a younger brother, however, whose name I have thankfully forgotten. Unfortunately, this young man viewed higher education in quite another way. He didn't study and he cheated when he could. He managed to guess right a few times, and somehow made it through his freshman year with a marginal record. He was on academic probation early in his sophomore year, but this didn't put a crimp in his social life. The proverbial push came to shove when he reached his final exam in American History. It was a big class, one of those one hundred-plus affairs in which the teacher didn't know anyone's name and only gave objective tests. Little Brother knew he couldn't pass the test; he had never opened the book and rarely ever went to class. He also knew that another "F" would put him out in the street, so he decided that brother Gordon would take the test for him. Gordon refused, and Little Brother failed.

Most of you are probably anticipating what happened next. You're betting Gordon said "No," creating friction between his brother and himself that would last a lifetime. But if this is what you expected then you've underestimated the problem—it was much, much worse.

When the family learned that the little brother was about to be bounced from the halls of academia, they joined forces and put the heat directly on Gordon! "How could you do this to your brother?!" they cried. Gordon felt rather strongly (and in my opinion, with complete justification) that little brother had brought this on himself. He flatly refused to bail out a lummox that was in a mess entirely of his own making. As expected, the Little Brother was expelled and spent the rest of his life blaming Gordon for not helping him in his hour of greatest need. The family agreed—forcing Gordon to fail the only test of his own academic career: the Allegiance Expectation.

The _Accommodation Expectation_ is based on the principle of rearranging space and time to meet the needs of relatives. When Aunt Mildred arrives unannounced from Peoria, a family member is expected to give her a place to stay. If Aunt Mildred brings Uncle Edgar and their four children, then perhaps two family members will be expected to open their homes. This continues with more and more homes being offered as the visiting wave grows. We saw a remarkable example of this earlier with Art and Marilyn. Family members are expected to be flexible in their schedules to accommodate the needs of their kin. Here's another example:

A young bachelor friend of mine, Chuck, was once told by the family elders that he was to "take in" a ne'er-do-well cousin who was getting out of prison and had no place to go. It was explained that "the boys" were about the same age, so it would be a Jim-Dandy living arrangement—as though they were about to start double-dating and joining the gang at the malt shop.

Chuck wanted no part of this because:

A) He liked living alone;
B) He had never liked the cousin, going back to their earliest childhood;
C) The man was a lifelong thief, and he didn't want to start hiding his wallet and his watch; and
D) He resented the decision being made without even being asked if he would do it.

Unlike some of the other people I have mentioned so far, Chuck is a man who has no trouble employing the word No, and he didn't agonize over this decision for as long as 30 seconds. In fact, the answer wasn't just "No," but *Hell No!* which carries the idea that it also applies to the future. I don't know what happened to the cousin, but Chuck went on living his happy bachelor life, the problem solved before it even had time to become a minor irritation. This is unquestionably the best way to handle any problem that must eventually be resolved by telling someone "No." Unfortunately, not everyone is a Chuck. Many people have great difficulty using their intellect to stand up to the old warriors who control the arsenals of emotion and expectation. Most of their stress comes from fear of *failing the test*, not in the fallout from the refusal. Therefore, people who know they should say "No" but do not will go on, year after year, giving in to family pressures and in the process, take another giant step each year toward the friendly neighborhood sanitarium.

✦ ✦ ✦

If I could sell my readers any message it would be this: learn to *say "No" when you need to.* Believe me, the world will not go to pieces when the word is spoken. On the contrary, it will become a brighter, happier place and you will have a lot more self-esteem.

Don't cave in to the emotional pressure heaped upon you by people who don't have the right to burden you with their problems or their guilt. When you give in to their demands you are playing their game. It's a poor coach who plays to another team's strength, and it makes no more sense in life than it does on the playing field.

You must also never lose sight of the fact that there is little happiness or personal satisfaction to be derived from giving in to avoid a fight. *Think about it!* Has giving in ever made you happy, cut down on stress, or created a better family relationship? Of course not. Giving in does nothing but placate the bully, justify the *you-owe-me* attitude, or encourage moochers and believers in their unreasonable expectations.

Remember, when it comes to dealing with difficult family situations you have two choices:

1) Live with them, or
2) Say "No" and get rid of them.

The second option makes a lot more sense.

Love and Marriage
(Intellect vs. Emotion)

> The tragedy of our age is that
> marriage is invariably emotional
> while divorce is logical.

It is impossible to get squared away on the subject of love and marriage without first comprehending the opposing forces of emotion and intellect. People who let their emotions rule them are in for a stormy and completely unsatisfactory love life.

In all things—and certainly in love and marriage—the intellect must rule the emotions. Think of your emotions as something like taking the dog out for a walk. The animal has a certain amount of freedom, but the leash keeps the animal under control. Let the dog have too much freedom, however, and the result is a dog running amok, following whatever fancy crosses its path while dragging you behind.

Very much to the point is the adage, "love is blind." This phrase exists because the majority of people enter marriage with the dog (their emotions) making all the decisions. Yet I can't think of a better reason to be ready with a firm "No!" than the life-altering consequences of marriage. I'm not saying you shouldn't marry—I'm saying you should put some real thought into who, why, and when you marry, and if the math doesn't add up, say "No."

Avoid Excessive Impulsiveness

Emotions are what make us love, hate, laugh, cry, sing, shout, and enjoy ourselves, but we should never allow them to control our choices. It's one thing to be impulsive—spontaneity adds spice to life—but even this must be in the context of an orderly life. It might be fun, for example, to fly away on an unplanned trip to Rio de Janeiro or Timbuktu, but only if the bills are paid and some money will still be in the bank when you return. Otherwise, this just creates a brand-new set of problems.

Impulsive people are almost always problem people. They pride themselves on what they perceive as their independence, often to the point of being monumental bores. But they're some of the first people to lean on others when the bills come due. I don't think I would find these people quite so offensive if they didn't spend so much time describing what irresponsible, devil-may-care scamps they really are and looking for our resultant admiration. As an entertainment device, I consider descriptions of impulsive exploits to be only one step ahead of war stories and vacation slides.

Impulsiveness is certainly not a desirable factor in the love-and-marriage department. While love is an admirable emotion, it must always be tempered with a generous supply of intellect. No matter how good the other person looks to you, the ultimate ideal in marriage is to spend a lifetime together. Remember, marriage doesn't solve anything. In fact it often causes more stress than it alleviates. For example, if you don't both work, your expenses suddenly double—but your income does not. Worse, if you are not compatible before marriage, the situation will not improve after marriage. Love and marriage are not magic, and you'll soon discover that bad habits become intolerable habits and weaknesses grow into major character defects. If you want to be happy in life, the intellect must take over before you marry, because a permanent arrangement must be based on something deeper than agitated glands.

It's OK to Say No!

The Intellect says "No"

Okay, so what does all this have to do with the word No? The answer is, *everything*. NO comes from the brain (the intellect), while YES is generally an emotional response (hence the ridiculous doctrine of Hedonism). For example:

- *Yes* tells us to drive home when we've had too much to drink; *No* tells us to call a cab.
- *Yes* tells us to charge an expensive item that we can't afford; *No* tells us not to buy it.
- *Yes* tells us to squeeze some more miles out of bald tires and bad brakes; *No* tells us to take care of the problem right away.
- *Yes* tells us to gamble with money we don't have; *No* tells us to avoid the risk.
- *Yes* sends us into marriages that haven't a chance of succeeding; *No* tells us to back off and find someone else.

To drive this last point home, it has been proven to my satisfaction that successful marriages are built on a commonality of background—on *compatibility*. This means that two Methodists from Mason City, Iowa, have a better chance of staying married than, say, a Roman Catholic from San Francisco and a Jehovah's Witness from Athens, Georgia. Intellectually, there's a small voice that tries to point out this obvious truth, but we often don't listen—usually because there's some idiot in our lives who invariably offers the worst advice in the world: *"Follow your heart."* And people usually follow it—all the way to the Divorce Court. When considering marriage, rule number one is that your intellect should be given more weight in the decision making process.

The Marital Veto Principle

Do you remember our discussion concerning obligation and responsibility in Chapter two? Based on that discussion, you're responsible for your own happiness, and that responsibility does not become your spouse's obligation once you're married. Indeed, once you're married, the word *No* comes into play in a way that can make your marriage work. I refer to what I humbly call *Smith's Marital Veto Principle*, which in my opinion forms the absolute bedrock for any successful marriage. In the Introduction, I noted that it is better to give up something we want than to have something thrust upon us that we don't want. This is the basis of the Marital Veto Principle.

There are many activities that married people often (even usually) do separately: shopping trips, football games, fashion shows, fishing, and so on. These do not fall into the domain of the Marital Veto Principle, which generally applies only to those activities that couples normally do together (unless, of course, you spend too much time watching football... but that's another issue). Under the terms of this principle, either party has the right to avoid an activity by just saying "No," and the other party is obligated to respect his or her wishes. Stated more simply, *No* almost always takes precedence over *Yes*.

The usual reaction to the Marital Veto Principle is the belief that it will negate all activities in common and basically dissolve a marriage without the benefit of a formal divorce. I'm quite sure that this objection comes from people who are accustomed to dragging their spouses to activities they don't enjoy. It doesn't have to be this way at all. Remember, if you did your homework and chose a compatible spouse, there are plenty of activities the two of you will enjoy doing together. If she can occasionally say "No" to him, and he can say "No" to her concerning those activities they don't share in common, they are casting out most of the unpleasantness in their marriage and leaving only the good things that make them happy.

This is much like the ancient American art of making corn whiskey. Barrels of mash are tossed into a frozen stream, the water and other nonalcoholic impurities freeze and the alcohol is forced to the center of the barrel, remaining in its liquid state.

The sludge (the painful, annoying things we don't want to do) is thrown away. The remaining alcohol (the sweet wonder of marriage) is combined in other barrels. The process is repeated, each time with more impurities being removed—the distiller and Mother Nature combining their talents until the end result is achieved: a barrel of smooth, sweet, pure corn whiskey (in my opinion, one of the premiere products ever to come out of the United States).

The Veto Principle uses the same type of refining process. With the constant removal of mandatory involvement with those people and events that bring displeasure to either of the marriage partners, each partner's interests are preserved—which alone is enough to make any marriage work. Neither party is dragged to anything they don't want to attend, and neither has to associate with people they consider offensive. The things they do together are things they both want to do. The result is like "pure moonshine in the final barrel." Pure bliss.

Maximizing Compatibility

The reason we need rules like Smith's Marital Veto Principle is because men and women do not really have a lot of built-in compatibility, and for this reason marriage must have everything possible working for it.

Regardless of the claims made by strong feminists, the male and female genders are coming from totally different places. They have deep-seated philosophic differences that exhibit themselves in many ways. For example, have you ever observed the two sexes on a house or apartment hunting expedition? It won't take more than a few minutes for you to note the differences. Women immediately head for the closets and cupboards, because these are important things to a woman. Men don't care one iota about closets and cupboards. Men look at the amount of space that will eventually need to be painted (stone and wood-paneled walls are a plus to a man) and whether the place is plumbed for a wet bar.

(I've had it explained to me at least a thousand times why closets and cupboards are essential to human existence, but I still can't work up any interest.)

Or have you ever noticed employees going to work in the morning? You will often see women arriving with gift-wrapped packages, but never men. Women are very big for exchanging gifts in the workplace. It would never have occurred to me (a one-time, so-called "gray suit") to bring a birthday gift for the guy at the next desk. It might even ruin a perfectly good friendship if I tried.

And have you ever listened to men and women talking to a painter? Women like subtlety in colors; for instance, "In this room I want just a hint of green just a teeny, teeny green cast—only a suggestion, a hint." A man would say, "Paint it green."

Then there's clothing. Women lean toward patterns that blend: a chocolate brown, for example, that blends into a light brown, then to a tan, then to beige, and eventually to white. A man would prefer a brown-and-white stripe. Whenever I see a man in a color-blended shirt, I know that his wife picked it out. And there's more:

- Women are better small talkers than men. Men are better than women at parking cars.
- Women are better at gift wrapping (or any kind of wrapping for that matter), but they are often poor map readers.
- Few women can make a decent martini, but women are better dancers than men and they're obviously better at growing indoor plants.

All of this is meant to establish the indisputable fact that men and women are basically different creatures. Neither is better nor worse, only different. They think differently, and they react differently to the same stimuli, which means that compatibility is not easily attained (but it's also why finding the right spouse results in a very strong union).

When two people embark on an essentially incompatible relationship that is based on nothing but emotion, the chances for survival are minimal at best. The only way that men and women can ever be passably compatible is for each to acquire a healthy respect for that magnificent word No.

There are many things that people simply have to do, unpleasant as they are. It is not particularly dangerous to the relationship when they are doing something that neither wants to do, such as a party at the boss' house, a business-related wedding they can't get out of, or maybe an obligatory visit to someone at the hospital. Compatibility does not suffer when neither person is enjoying the occasion and they have a common interest in ducking out early. It is only when one has been constantly dragged somewhere that the relationship suffers, and this is where the word No becomes effective.

(However, we cannot discount the fact that there will occasionally be activities such as family gatherings that require both partners to be present, even if one partner would rather be somewhere else. But again, if you have chosen your partner wisely— using your intellect more than your emotions—these occasions will be rare.)

Testing Compatibility

Now that I've established just how critical compatibility is, let's return for a moment to the time before you got married. I think any rational person would agree that men and women have to meet on an intellectual plane if there is to be any kind of worthwhile coexistence. Passion is good for a three or four week run, but there comes a time when one partner makes an intelligible statement and the other is expected to reply. The day inevitably arrives when the bloom is off the rose. Couples who thought about their partners and planned their marriages well will be able to settle down into a happy and companionable coexistence. Couples who made choices based on hormones will discover a life full of misery and pain. (Hollywood marriages are a better than average example.)

> People with good sense are discriminating in their tastes and find it difficult to accept the unacceptable. Intelligent people reject, but fools never do.

It must be a terribly traumatic experience to complete a year or two of married life and then realize that you are pledged into eternity with a complete imbecile. I'm not afraid to say that highly emotional people often lean toward imbecility, because they tend to be nonselective and are often unable to discriminate between good and bad—between quality and garbage. When I hear a person described as someone who "likes everything," I immediately envision someone with an IQ of about 15—a "good sport" who has trouble holding a fork.

Shifting the Emphasis

Because compatibility is geared for the long run, I have often thought that the emphasis in marriage should be shifted from the wedding celebration to the first anniversary. A wedding is too often nothing more than a manifestation of physical attraction, even when the participants are already living together. A shared living arrangement where "either of us can walk out if it doesn't work" involves no commitment; only in a legally binding marriage do two people learn if they have the maturity, the compassion, and the intelligence to make it over the long haul. Therefore, I think that the wedding should be simple and the big bash reserved for the first anniversary. The first year is much more significant than the engagement, and those twelve months successfully spent together are more worthy of celebration than the wedding itself.

My good friend, the Sage of Bakersfield, is in favor of a premarital test much like the test we give for U.S. citizenship. Before he married his second wife, he asked her to name the capital of all 50 states and the names of the last three vice-presidents. She passed the test, even though she had no idea that her impending marriage was riding on the results. (The Sage's first wife thought Seattle was the capital of Oregon, and this soured the relationship considerably.) The Sage's second marriage has worked out quite well, however, so he created a 60-question test to be given to individuals before they marry, with the recommendation that only two "passers" (or two "failers") should marry each other. Although he says he wouldn't spend his life with anyone less than a "55," he considers 45 to be a passing grade. In his opinion, anyone who scores less than 45 is not only not worth marrying, he or she is not worth knowing. But that's another issue.

The first 50 questions comprise a list of all states in the United States—from Alaska to Wyoming—with the goal being to name the capital of each one. This is followed by:

- Who invented the telephone?
- If you knew the diameter of a circle, how would you find its circumference?
- Who was the first Vice-President of the United States?
- Who wrote *For Whom The Bell Tolls?*
- Which two states are the largest in area and in population? (No half-point credit on this one.)
- What is the first book of the Holy Bible?
- What subject would you be studying if you had to memorize Faraday's Law?
- Who represents your district in Congress?
- Name one ballet composed by Tchaikovsky.
- What is the capital of Canada?

Although the Sage doesn't envision this test ever being backed with the force of law, he does consider it to be an excellent guide for anyone who is contemplating matrimony: a simple case of knowing what one is getting.

I think that the real value of premarital testing is in the admonition that only passers and failers should marry each other. Two lunkheads who can't even name their own state capital will probably be quite compatible. All they need is a six-pack, *The National Enquirer,* and each other, and they'll achieve total bliss. The only

It's OK to Say No!

thing that could ever befoul this "Edenic" situation is if one of them decided to take a class or in any way seek intellectual improvement.

At the other end of the spectrum, two bright people who share an awareness of the world around them also have a good chance of making it together. "Cross-breeding," however, is a dangerous business at best.

> When two fools marry, they owe it to each other to remain fools.

Bright people should never marry imbeciles, no matter how strong the physical attraction. (Sorry, guys, no trophy wives!). All that anyone can ever expect in this situation is a one-night stand and a pleasant memory.

Love Should Never Be Blind

You'll remember from Chapter One that it was back in the 1950s when the Positive Thinking twaddle started making inroads into the American psyche. It was inevitable that it would invade the love/marital relationship as well. The result is a tendency for people to turn a blind eye to the problems in their marriage—a willingness to chant, "Our marriage is good! Our marriage is good!" despite all evidence to the contrary.

To educated and intelligent men and women, it is obvious why Positive Thinking is seductive to people in a bad marriage. As common as divorce is, it's still embarrassing. There's a social stigma attached to people who can't work out their differences. Worse, there's enormous social pressure to *make marriage work*, which in my mind is a pompous way of saying, "You made your bed, now lie in it!" The result is that people (usually wives) will do anything to keep a bad marriage together—to turn a blind eye to the realities of their relationship.

Like any other human activity, marriages are fueled by the force of reality. One starts by seeing the intended mate for who and what he or she is, accepting the appraisal as an immutable fact of life, and then going on from there.

I once worked with a man named Bill who was quite good at his job and for the most part, a likable person. Unfortunately, he had a drinking problem, and over a period of several years I watched the problem grow. His ever-faithful and loving wife, Linda, was the positive thinker to end all positive thinkers, and she wasn't about to see the dark side of anything. This woman was so perpetually cheerful, in fact, that I found it difficult to spend much time with her. My own wife and I saw Bill and Linda at many social functions, and they all ended the same way. Bill was bombed halfway through the evening, and Linda had to drive home. There were also the unfailing excuses: Bill hasn't eaten since breakfast; Bill didn't get any sleep last night and he's soooo tired; Bill has been under a lot of stress; Bill is taking medication, and he shouldn't have had a drink. She always avoided the obvious issue.

Everyone else in the room knew exactly what the problem was. Bill was a lush, and the one thing that Bill did not need was the kind of "support" his wife was giving him. He didn't need (and shouldn't have had) the constant cover-up. What Bill needed was a loud, unmistakable, *No!* to his drinking. (Their marriage was definitely not an example of how a healthy marriage should work.)

This brings us back to compatibility. There is a certain *rightness* to the male–female relationship that is essential if anything good is to ever come from it. Linda and Bill were not *right* for each other. She ignored the obvious, despite the fact that Bill desperately needed help with his drinking problem. The positive-thinking, go-for-it approach to love and romance ignores the need for *rightness* in the relationship, which is why married people cheat and single people lie to each other. It is a matter of staging a play that cannot exist outside the theater.

Lest we be confused, *rightness* has nothing to do with the similar-sounding *righteousness*. *Rightness* exists when two compatible people are free to enter a romantic relationship and are honest with each other. If she has a child that he doesn't know about, or if he has a prison record that she doesn't suspect, then there is obviously something lacking in the rightness department. *Righ-*

teousness, on the other hand, is defined in terms of beliefs and philosophy, and changes from one religion or philosophy to the next (which is a pretty good reason why Christians and Muslims probably shouldn't marry).

The old "I'll-marry-you-when-the-kids-are-grown" routine doesn't fit the pattern, either. In this scenario, one person is lying while the other is a willing participant in an adulterous relationship. What good can come from it? What worthy woman would believe such a moldy old line in the first place? It's akin to the old Groucho Marx line, "I wouldn't belong to any organization that would have me as a member." Applying this to the love-and-marriage scene, a man might be heard to say, "I wouldn't marry anyone so dumb that she believes the line I'm using to get her into bed."

◆ ◆ ◆

Now that we have covered the manner in which two people should act toward each other, we should look at their relationships with other people. There is probably no more significant line in the traditional marriage vow than "forsaking all others," which means that the married couple's interests come first—always, forever, and into eternity. Putting an outsider's interests over those of one's mate is just as great a violation of the marriage vows as adultery and desertion would be.

To put it succinctly, a married person's first loyalty, first duty, and first responsibility is to his or her spouse. Other people get what is leftover, if anything. If this sounds a bit harsh, then reverse it and see if the words sound right: the spouse gets what's leftover. Do you like that one better?

Remember that money, time, and attention are limited resources. Those who make demands upon others are usually looking for a place on someone's ladder of priorities—they want a portion of their limited resources. In marriage, we don't play for a tie. The husband and wife are always first, everyone else is second. This is not only the way it is, but the way it *has to be*. (As the line goes, "forsaking all others." If you agree to it, then mean it.)

It's OK to Say No!

In order to put one's mate first, it is often necessary to invoke the most beneficent of all words—the word *No.* Let's look at one example. Bart and Maxine had been married for three years and lived all of that time in Los Angeles. They had wanted to go to Paris on their honeymoon but couldn't afford it, so they spent the three years saving for their dream trip. They called it their Three-Year-Plan. Through careful management they saved enough for the trip, and right on schedule, they were ready to go. Bart was looking forward to the trip, but his enthusiasm paled when compared to Maxine's. She was ecstatic over the thought of it. *Paris!*

About a month before they were to leave, however, Bart received a phone call at work from his sister. She told him about a big family reunion in Nebraska, and Bart was to schedule his vacation accordingly. The plan was to rent a van, and the California contingent (eight people in all) would travel *en masse* to meet the others in Nebraska. Relatives were coming from all directions and, oh! wasn't it going to be fun?

Bart told her about the trip to Paris, and that he couldn't get another vacation for a whole year, and that Maxine had her heart set on going, and so on. But his sister would have none of it. "You can go to Paris any time," she said. "But the family might never get together again." In his sister's mind, it had already been decided: Bart and Maxine were as good as in the van and speeding toward the Great Plains.

It was now crunch time for Bart. He waffled at first and said that he'd get back to her as soon as he could "clear up a few things." When he put down the phone, he intended to call Maxine and explain the situation; but then, in one of those marvelous revelations that come so seldom in a lifetime, he realized what it meant to be married. He realized what his responsibilities were to his wife as opposed to the obligation his sister assumed he had to his family. Bart called his sister back and told her flatly and irrevocably, "No." He and his wife were going to Paris, and that was the end of it.

It's OK to Say No!

His sister was terribly upset. His brother-in-law didn't care much one way or the other, and several aunts and uncles wondered what was becoming of the younger generation. They couldn't understand why a young couple would rather visit Paris than pitch horseshoes in a Nebraskan beanfield. A big rift developed between Bart and his family that never has quite healed, but he did what had to be done and his marriage is stronger for it. It was quite significant, I thought, that he didn't even tell Maxine about the family reunion until they returned from the trip. Paris meant so much to her that he didn't want a load of guilt and anger to be carried on her shoulders to the banks of the Seine. After that, it wouldn't really matter anyway.

There was actually a bigger issue at stake here than simply Paris versus Nebraska. The sister had said that they could go to Paris next year, but was this really true? If his family could cancel the trip once, they could do it again. A priority would have been established. Bart and Maxine could have gone to Paris next year *only* if Bart's family allowed it.

As I think about the situation now, I have to equate it with the real meaning of marriage. Often, people actually *marry* long after the legal wedding date. In this case, the true marriage began when Bart got back on the phone and told his sister that he and Maxine were going to Paris. That is the precise moment when his wife became the top priority in his value system.

It shouldn't surprise you that setting priorities correctly is a function of intellect, not emotion. People who follow their emotions will very likely wind up in the divorce court, jail, or the hospital. People who think about the decisions they make are very likely to end up prosperous, content, and above all, happy.

The best advice that anyone can give to someone who is contemplating marriage is to be hard-headed and analytical. Use the same logic that you would use to buy common stock or to shop for a transmission overhaul. Forget that nonsense about mythical bells ringing and ask if this is the right person for you—not just someone who agitates your hormones, but a person with whom you plan to go to PTA meetings and Little League games, make mortgage payments, share a bathroom, and worry about the crabgrass. Even in love, a person is well advised to follow the dictates of the brain rather than the glands. After all, the brain is the one organ in the body that will never steer you wrong.

The Retirement Years
(Self-Interest vs. Selfishness)

> If you really don't want to do it,
> don't.

There is certainly no period of our lives that we should dedicate more to our personal happiness than the golden years of retirement. This is when we can shed many of the responsibilities of our youth and begin living the way we've always wanted to live. Unfortunately, it is also the time of life when many of us become "patsies," easy marks for unscrupulous opportunists, needy family members, and well-meaning friends. It is a time when the daughter comes home, bringing her children with her; when the son needs immediate cash to get himself out of a mess that he alone created; or when someone decides that the retiree has "plenty of time" to spare and tries to consume most of it. Far too often, it is a time when all of the unhappiness we've been discussing since the beginning of this book becomes manifest.

Servicing Self-Interest

Too often, we confuse self-interest with selfishness, and retirement is definitely a time when self-interest must be served. Unlike younger people, retirees don't get another shot at it. Whatever they have is the result of a lifetime of planning, and they cannot go back and recoup their losses. For retirees, a loan is money that probably isn't going to be repaid; it is gone, lost, down the sewer, because time is on the side of the borrower.

The person who needs a legitimate loan (for a correspondingly legitimate purpose) goes to a bank or some other lending institution with every expectation of repaying the money on a predetermined schedule—while those who back relatives into a corner and ask for money are rarely good credit risks. They know full well that they are asking for money that is generally already invested and constitutes part of the retiree's income. Nonetheless, repayment is usually expressed in terms of, "when I get back on my feet," which bears a close resemblance to, "wait 'til the sun shines, Nellie," and is about as specific.

Retirement is especially difficult for those people who have traditionally been the repository for other people's problems—the old *dumper-dumpee* game from Chapter 3. Dumpers are notorious for believing that someone's retirement gives them license to start dumping again (or even more than before), as if the retiree has magically gained time and money that's burning a hole in his or her pocket.

> When a worker receives a gold watch and a farewell dinner, it should be understood that he is off-limits to poachers, and is an endangered species among humankind.

I remember a situation many years ago involving Joe and Martha, a couple who were friends of my parents. In fact, their problem was the single event in my life that influenced my thinking along the lines of enlightened pragmatism and would eventually form the framework for most of my writing.

As I recall, I was about 14 years old when I first heard my parents talking about "poor Joe." It seems Joe retired after forty years of employment with a public utility company and planned to spend his retirement years traveling and indulging his life's passion— amateur archaeology (a passion his wife, Martha, was happy to share). Unfortunately, Martha's sister and her husband (who had

It's OK to Say No!

just lost his job—again) decided to move in with them to cut down on expenses. Something was said about Joe and Martha having "plenty of room" (it wasn't Joe and Martha who said it) and the in-laws took up residence—with Joe as the sole support of the household. Shortly after that, the new tenants' daughter left her husband and also moved in, only compounding the situation.

When I heard about all this, my adolescent mind looked for a single solution. I wondered why Joe couldn't have just barred the door and said something like, "No, you aren't moving in." I was told that "things just weren't that simple," and that I would understand when I was an adult.

Well, now I'm an adult, and I still don't understand why Joe was required to support that pack of deadbeats. He continued as the sole provider for this brood until he died seven years later. The declining years of his life, which could and should have been happy and perhaps somewhat prolonged, were bent to the will of thoughtless people who would have considered Joe to be incredibly selfish had he said "No" when they initially took advantage of his good nature (and his obvious aversion to confrontation).

This case is merely one variation among thousands that are happening all over this country. Someone is deemed to have "a big house" or "plenty of time and money," and *Zap!* Here come the marching locusts, ready for a feast. Retirees are especially susceptible because they're often seen as having "made it." They obviously have the time, the money, and certainly the desire to help . . . right?

Joe and Martha had invested wisely and planned for retirement. They were ready for those golden years, only the "gold" was snatched from them. They forgot that it is essential to one's self-interest that marching locusts be met and repulsed. A retiree has the right to think of the rest of his or her life as something sacred and inviolable. It is a simple case of saying, "It's mine, I earned it through hard work, and you can't have it!"

Compassion Should Not Be Extorted

This should *not* be interpreted to mean that retirement is a time when a person turns his back on the world. Remember, the issue here is self-interest, not selfishness. The distinction to be made is between time and money freely given to people in need and back-against-the-wall extortion by people who think it's only fair that we share. Unfortunately, it often seems easier to give in and come across with the loot than to tell somebody to "get lost." The operative word here is *seems,* because we're dealing with an illusion. Paying off might make the immediate problem go away, but it will be back again tomorrow. The permanent solution is the word No, and it's also a lot cheaper.

Giving, helping, and caring are voluntary things. I have known more than one retired couple who willingly dug into their saddlebags and helped their children make down payments on that first house, or gave grandchildren financial packages to put them through college. These are great things, and they're not what this chapter is about. It's really about staying out of the net cast by someone else's self-interest, and never being trapped into doing something you don't want to do.

Knowing When to Say No

Henri Amiel said, "To know how to grow old is the master-work of wisdom, and one of the most difficult chapters in the great art of living." These are wise words indeed. I especially like the phrase about knowing "how to grow old;" there is a definite knack to it. Some people are terrible at this, while others glide into it with all the grace of a gazelle and then wear age like a well-tailored suit. There's an important corollary to Amiel's statement, however. One must have the opportunity to exercise his or her knowledge—and this is where the word *No* comes into the picture.

I received a lot of mail in the years immediately after my book, *How to Cure Yourself of Positive Thinking,* was published. In fact, I still correspond with several of these people. One letter came from a widower named Doug who lives in Tucson, Arizona. He had read my book and seemed to regard the discovery that he could say "No" as some kind of personal awakening or revelation. I was gratified that I could help him live a happier life, but I was especially interested in his particular problem because it was a primary example of a situation that had grown to stressful proportions because of indecision and inaction. Doug's problem was brought about by well-meaning friends, all of whom lived in his condominium complex. For months, they were determined to "fix him up" with a widow who also lived there. He had no interest in the woman at all; in fact, he didn't even want her as a friend, much less romantically. He found her to be dull-witted and completely uninteresting, and he was bored into a semi-comatose condition whenever he found himself (however briefly) in her company.

His friends persisted, though, and invited him to all kinds of social functions where he and the widow would be the only single people present. The lady was reported to be quite interested in him, so there was no problem getting her to cooperate. She attended each function and kept tossing her net into the water. For their part, the friends kept saying how much he and the lady had in common, always prefacing the perceived commonality with the expression, "You two . . . ." For his part, he saw little similarity beyond the fact that they both had ten fingers, ten toes, and were air-breathing mammals.

He tried to explain this, but his friends would have none of it. And this is where he made his mistake: he kept skirting the problem rather than facing and eliminating it. To avoid the situation, he filled his social calendar with things that kept him "busy" and unavailable at all times, even though they were things that he didn't particularly want to do. He also did whatever he could to avoid any face-to-face encounters with his old friends (by now his tormentors).

I am proud to say that after reading my book, this man saw the light. Bells rang and the mental gears meshed. He finally realized that there was no need to avoid his old friends and no need to keep on being "busy," especially when it meant spending his time in pursuits with nothing going for them except that they were better than the alternative. He invited the five worst offenders (three women and two men) to his home one evening, served a round of drinks to create an air of cordiality, and then got on with business by delivering the following terse message:

"I have no interest in knowing Mrs. so-and-so, even as a friend, and I am asking all of you to cease in your efforts to bring us together. I am tired of making excuses and avoiding all of you, nor should it be necessary. We will now meet the problem head-on, and you are the problem. To put it succinctly—stop it!"

There were some bruised feelings for awhile, of course. The problem came to an abrupt end, however, and everything soon returned to normal. He went on to enjoy his retirement, and was kind enough to recommend my book to anyone who had trouble saying "No." (*How to Cure Yourself of Positive Thinking* sold rather well in Tucson, so there must have been some problems in that area.)

If we analyze the situation with any degree of intensity, we see several factors that are common to so many of our personal problems. First, there really shouldn't have been a problem at all. Doug allowed it to exist and even helped it along by his inaction. He should have gone to the host and hostess the day after the first *special pairing* with the widow was arranged and made it absolutely clear that he objected to such manipulation, and that it wasn't to happen again.

Second, he spent too much time worrying about the feelings of those people who quite obviously hadn't stopped to consider his. "Well-meaning" friends often are not well-meaning at all; in fact, the term is almost an oxymoron. Whenever it is used, a story of someone who completely mucked up a situation and hurt someone in the process usually follows.

Finally, Doug deluded himself into believing that a problem ignored is a problem solved. It isn't. Problems have remarkable staying power, and they're always waiting for you when you wake up in the morning.

I like Doug's example because it is so typical of a universal problem. This was a relatively minor situation—little more than an irritant—that grew into something major because of a reluctance to say "No." In this case, our man found himself inventing excuses, slipping out his own door at odd hours like a criminal, avoiding his old friends, and generally creating a lot of stress for himself. It wasn't necessary. It could have been easily avoided by saying the magic word. (By now, I think we all know what that word is.)

Only You Can Determine What Is in Your Best Self-Interest

Our British cousins use a phrase—"the prime of life"—to describe the retirement years, and it is most appropriate. Although some people elect to waste this great experience by growing old too soon and then whining because of fancied slights from the younger generation, most see the over-60 life as a shot at freedom. They are anxious to do all of those things there just wasn't time for when raising a family and scratching out a living.

Unfortunately, as noted at the beginning of this chapter, there are also many people who see retirees as a mark and who aim all guns in their direction. To the Problem Perennial, the retiree represents the Holy Grail, the Golden Fleece, El Dorado, and the Emerald City, all rolled into one ripe-for-the-picking package. It is an unfortunate rule of life that if anyone is even assumed to possess a bit of spare cash, spare time, or spare energy, *someone* is going to ask for it.

Most retirees are quite unprepared for the role of pigeon. Responsible people invest their money, cover themselves with medical and dental insurance, if necessary move to more affordable housing, and plan for just about every facet of retirement living. They do not, however, plan

> True friendship is based on a lack of assumptions.

on the big bite, that unexpected relative or old acquaintance who is going to sweep down like a giant bird of prey and want a piece of a good thing. Usually, the bite is predicated on the assumption that the retiree is both willing and able to absorb the incursion. ("What the hell, George and Mabel can afford it. They're loaded." Or perhaps, "They have time on their hands. They can baby-sit a couple of times a week.") It is an assumption that the Problem Perennial has no right to make, but makes anyway.

I have always been an advocate of living defensively, and this attitude is particularly valuable for those who have reached retirement age. This is the time to raise the drawbridge, circle the wagons, man the parapets, and issue extra ammunition to the troops. The enemy is out there, and he is going to hit every weak spot in the lines. Prepare for action and hold your ground.

> When we look for symbols in the animal world, let's forget the eagle and the lion, because defense is the key to life. Our standards should feature the cornered rat. Here we have a survivor.

There are those who would find a lot of paranoia in these words, but that is only a superficial analysis. Paranoia is a delusion, an irrational fear, and those very real people who stand on your doorstep with their luggage are not flights of fancy. The guy with his hand out for part of your pension is not a phantom.

To step gracefully into the retirement years, retirees would be well-advised to follow several basic rules, preferably beginning at the precise moment that retirement commences. In fact, it wouldn't be a bad idea for them to start practicing a few months before, so their reactions will come more easily later on. These "golden" rules are:

1. Accept the indisputable fact that someone thinks you are a mark.
2. Jealously guard your money and your time.
3. Let your good works be voluntary. All giving must originate with you.
4. Do not compromise your own security for anyone.

5. Learn to anticipate a touch for a loan.
6. Never allow yourself to be backed into a corner. Never commit to anything without first taking time to contemplate the consequences.
7. Never respond to somebody else's self-made problem.
8. Practice saying "No" until it comes easily.

It is essential that the retiree be ultraconservative with time and money because there will never be time to win them back. The days of risk-taking end with retirement. There isn't time to speculate, nor should it even be considered. People who planned wisely can coast on whatever they have, but they cannot take on an extra load. Personal security (a/k/a, *self-interest*) must be guarded jealously, even selfishly.

In regard to item No. 7—*responding to someone else's self-made problem*—retirees should recognize that there is no way of keeping up with a person who is going to jump back into the same mess after every bailout. The gambler and the drinker, for example, are going to be in trouble forever unless *they* do something about their problems. People looking for a way to get rich quick and traffic violators fall into the same category. Helping these people is not like jump-starting a neighbor's car on a cold morning or babysitting for a friend in an emergency. Their needs are never-ending, and you could make a career out of saving these Problem Perennials. It is one thing to argue that these people have a disease (which I question), but if so, it is a disease that people in their retirement years do not need to share and are certainly not responsible to cure. Retirees need these people in their lives like they need new wrinkles on their faces or more arthritis in their feet.

My wife and I had some neighbors once whose daughter married (over their strong objections) an imbecile who had dropped out of school, worked only on occasion, and took great pleasure in dispensing corporal punishment. Periodically, the daughter would appear on their doorstep with various abrasions, contusions, and lacerations, then stake a claim on her old room. "This time" (she claimed) she had "left him for good!" But when the wounds were healed, she would predictably go back to the imbecile. ("I love him, and I know that he loves me.") Then the cycle would start all over again. This situation was chronic, and the problem never ended. (Remember a similar scenario from Chapter 4?)

This problem did not belong to the young woman's parents, but they were included because of her assumption that they would or should share their resources with her—despite the fact that the problem was of her own making. As far as I know, this sad merry-go-round is still going on (assuming that the imbecile hasn't killed her by this time). It gives pause when you consider what a well-placed "No" could have accomplished in the lives of this girl and her parents.

Finally, a parting word about rule #8—*Practice saying "No" until it comes easily*. Retirees would do well to make the word No a part of everyday living, like buttering toast or checking the thermostat. Equally important, however, is meaning it when you say it and being ready to back it up. Remember that this word is to be used as though it were carved in stone, with no retreat and no negotiation. Your retirement years can be the high point of your life or the ultimate in human misery. It is entirely up to you to protect your self-interest and drive the snakes from the garden.

Learn It Young!

> No one ever reached maturity
> through perpetual concurrence.

I've spent a fair amount of time demonstrating just a few of the reasons why the world would be a better place and we'd be happier if we would just start saying "No!" During the next three chapters I want to spend some time discussing *how* to say "No," and there's no better place to start than at the beginning—which means starting young.

Indeed, I sincerely hope to catch just one generation on its way up and offer a few tips (dare I say a *program*) on how to live a happy life. These few rules should lessen considerably our teenagers' chances of permanent residency in a prison or a mental institution, and if they're willing to listen, *someday* (as the old cliché goes) *they'll thank me.*

So boys and girls, this chapter's for you—while there's still some hope of prying you loose from the never-be-selfish, you've-always-gotta-help-your-jailbird-brother dogma you've been taught your whole life. Don't let it get an iron grip on you. If you can recognize this nonsense for what it is and discard it before it does any permanent damage, there's still a chance to spare you a lifetime of bad decisions, unnecessary trauma, and debilitating unhappiness.

Simply put, I want to wean you away from the emotional thinking that is so damaging to a useful and productive life. If reading my previous chapters has not convinced you, then I can only ask that you trust me when I say, "People who make decisions with their glands rather than their brains are guaranteed to be miserable." Unfortunately, every generation has to learn this simple truth—over and over again.

With this in mind, let me introduce you to some simple rules that will bring happiness into your life.

Never Enter a Battle You Can't Win

Adherents of the Positive Thinking philosophy will never tell you this, but some battles really are lost before you ever pick up the gun. There just isn't any point in marching off to war when there's nothing left to win. Here's one example:

Dewey and Louie are contending for a promotion at their work. Only one position is available. As soon as one of them gets the promotion (let's say Dewey wins), you can be assured that some idiot will advise Louie to march into the superior's office and demand to know why he didn't get the job. This is absolutely the wrong thing to do because the boss doesn't want his or her authority challenged and will resent the confrontation. The boss will not and cannot admit to a wrong decision (which probably wasn't the case anyway) and the challenger will accomplish nothing except to emerge as a complete fool.

Once the decision was made, the case was closed. It became a no-win situation for Louie. He should have accepted the decision and moved on to better things.

Complaining when we're audited by the IRS is another no-win situation, as is getting upset when we're rudely dumped by a romantic partner. Getting argumentative in this latter situation will only create more animosity, and pleading never accomplished anything. (Revenge is always a possibility if one goes in for that sort of thing, but it generates problems of its own.) The simple fact is, dumping is usually forever—which leads to my first rule:

Rule #1: *stop complaining in no-win situations and move on to something productive.*

Use Your Head When Choosing a Mate

I spent an entire chapter on this, but it's worth reiterating. Marriage really isn't something you should be doing again and again throughout your life because starting over with a new companion does not get easier as you get older.

My advice, regardless of your gender, is to look for someone with reasonably good sense: the more intelligent the better. There can be no hell greater than life with an idiot. The pleasure of physical attraction <u>will</u> wear thin after a time (like over a weekend) but intelligence has a degree of permanence that you can enjoy throughout your life.

Women and Marriage

Ladies, go ahead and date the football hero or the "Big Man On Campus," but when you start thinking of marriage, *go for the nerd.* Believe me, most of the successful men in the world—the movers and shakers and people who make things happen—were probably nerds in high school. Many of them even carried sunglasses and calculators in their pocket protectors. I wish I could show you the wonderful pro-school commercial made by Teri Garr many years ago. "Do you remember the nerds you knew in school?" she asked. "Do you know what they're doing today? *They're doing anything they want!*"

The truth is, the teenage nerd is already far more mature than the campus big shots, the ones who wear the right clothes, use the right language, and move with the assurance of people who have all the answers. The nerd observes this childish routine but can't work up any enthusiasm for it because it registers as immature and trivial in his mind. His attention is directed toward science, music, investments, or maybe the mastery of foreign languages. The one thing that no one ever foresees about the nerd is that at the twentieth class reunion, he will probably be able to buy and sell everyone in the room. Thus:

Rule #2 (for the ladies): date the jocks if you want, but marry the nerds.

Men and Marriage

Now that I'm no longer a teenager I can finally admit the truth—the most popular girl on campus is usually an airhead. In the adult world, intelligence and popularity are not particularly compatible, but in adolescence they sit on different sides of a vast chasm. Young men rarely realize that cuteness is a transitory thing, while intelligence and maturity (like diamonds) are forever. Never forget that marriage lasts a lot longer than a short ride on the homecoming float. Married people still have to communicate. A good marriage is two people who turn to each other for advice, exchange opinions, and generally help each other become better people. Growing old is a difficult experience under any circumstance, but the problem is compounded tenfold when one marches hand-in-hand with a spouse who never outgrew her Barbie Doll attitude.

The women men should be looking for are the sensible ones—those who take the time to study and prepare themselves for the future. They might not be the best dancers, and they might not be the most popular girls in town, but do you remember the adage, "behind every good man . . . ?" It's far more important for a man to marry a woman who can help him make his dreams come true than a woman who only serves as window dressing.

Rule #2 (for the men): date the airheads if you must, but marry the girls who can help you succeed in life.

Do Not Even Consider a Nonmarital Living Arrangement

The issue of nonmarital living arrangements has a lot to do

with emotion vs. intellect and my previous discussions on marriage. The argument always made for "living together" is that if it doesn't work out, both parties can simply walk away and no one is hurt. This never happens, however, because the argument is based on the supposition that both parties will come to that realization at the same time. Life just isn't that tidy. The most common ending is that one person walks, and the other is dumped. Marriages, friendships, business relationships—literally all relationships we have in life—frequently break apart due to controversy, stress, or anger. This is *reality*.

To make matters worse, a shack-up (or an "extended one night stand," if you prefer) represents the worst of both worlds: both married life and single life. It lacks the respectability and commitment of marriage, yet eliminates the freedom of being single. People who live together do not date other people—at least not openly—and they're still required to call home when they aren't going to make it for dinner.

Because there is no binding marital contract in live-in situations, there's no sense of responsibility or true unity. Both partners feel that they can break the relationship whenever they want because there's nothing tying them together except their emotions—and judging by the number of unmarried couples that *don't* stay together, most nonmarital relationships are doomed to failure. I simply cannot imagine why any single person would willingly opt for this no-win situation. My advice is to go for the fulfillment of a traditional marriage—or stay single and swing. Don't settle for the worst of both worlds.

Rule #3: Act responsibly; either commit to marriage, or commit to being single.

Listen to People Who Know More than You

There is probably no bigger falsehood dropped on American youth than the nonsense that they have to "learn from experience." Experience is a very poor teacher. It's the single most inefficient way to learn anything (well, maybe other than placing a textbook under your pillow). I have never understood the necessity of spending days or weeks learning something that could easily be explained in ten minutes by someone who has already gained knowledge on the subject.

The old "you must gain your own experience" hogwash is invariably pushed by people who don't like to read and were extremely poor students. The person who says, "You just can't learn that in a book," is usually someone who has never *read a* book and hasn't the foggiest idea of what can and cannot be learned from a printed page. When you want to know something that you don't already know, either find an author who is an expert on the subject or talk to someone with some demonstrated skill in that area.

Experience represents the hard way of learning anything. It is the armor of the incompetent, the saber of the unlettered, and is always recommended by people who don't know any other way. These are people who would have to jump off a building to find out that it hurts. The best approach to learning is to listen to the masters. You can always hire people with "experience"; they come cheap.

Rule #4: learn from the people who already have the answers.

Don't Be Talked into Taking Foolish Risks

There are *some* risks to almost everything we do, but use your best judgment and keep the risks to a minimum (certainly less than you can afford to lose). One of the great myths of our time is that one has to take risks to make money (usually rendered, "you need to spend money to make money"). This is a vast oversimplification. Wheelers and dealers make money by letting *other people* take the risks. They let the suckers put up the money, then cash in when there's a profit to be made. They push this risk principle because they want someone else (you, for example) to put up the money for their shaky deals.

Investing is like dieting. There's only one effective way to lose

74   It's OK to Say No!

weight: eat right and exercise. Fads may work for a few people, but that's the exception, not the rule. The same is true for making money. The way to wealth is through patient, sound investment. Learn something about economics at an early age (now, for example), and listen to people with a demonstrated ability to acquire wealth. The clown with the big mouth and holes in his shoes is always available to tell you how to make that big score, but all that you have to do is look at him. If he knew anything about making money, he would be rich.

Never—I repeat, *never*—go along with any scheme that mentions "getting in on the ground floor." Look for something that is already well established because it has a demonstrated ability to rise. I recommend putting your money on the "floor just below the top," riding it up a notch, and then going back for another helping. This reminds me of what is perhaps the most succinct statement I have yet heard on the accrual of wealth. The esteemed financier Barnard Baruch was once asked for the secret of his financial success. His reply? "Selling too soon." And while we're on the subject, let me mention a word or two about *greed*. As a Californian, I am quite familiar with the lore of the "Gold Rush," which has been romanticized to the point of nausea. The truth is that it was based entirely on greed and it featured a pack of idiots charging westward with no knowledge of gold mining, all looking to make that big score. Very few of them ever made a profit, because there wasn't enough gold to make it worthwhile for a tenth of the horde that went there. Most of the gold miners ended up poor, destitute, or dead. The only real money that was made out of the Gold Rush (and this is very important!) went to the *merchants* in San Francisco and Sacramento, the men and women who were selling the miners their shovels and axes. Hardware is a solid business; gold panning is not.

> When the subject is making money, only the rich man is an expert.

The sad fact is that if another gold rush happened anywhere in the world, the same thing would happen again. The get-rich-quick crowd would do all of the work, while people with the good sense to supply them with food and equipment would make a tidy profit.

Money is made with minimal risk, maximum patience, and a sound knowledge of what you are doing. The beauty of it all is that so few people are willing to believe this, there isn't much competition. So go get it. The world is well stocked with fools who are dedicated to making *you* rich.

Rule #5: Don't take foolish risks.

Reject All Forms of Positive Thinking

As I've described in earlier chapters, Positive Thinking is a philosophy for people with nothing else going for them. It is a lot of half-mystical nonsense based on the premise that all kinds of "good things" will happen if you just get the Positive Thinking juices flowing. Believe me, you don't need this kind of bilge water to be successful. Real, predictable success is built on preparation, hard work, and consistency.

Positive Thinking can also be thought of as a rain dance philosophy. It tries to tie a successful conclusion to a totally unrelated effort. It is about a quarter-cut above astrology in having any scientific justification, and it should be treated in about the same way. You can look for measurable results from some form of illusory foot shuffling, or you can step into the real world and *make* things happen. Just keep in mind that the old adage is true: "Pray like everything depends on God, then work like everything depends on you!"

Rule #6: Avoid the Positive Thinking mentality. Stop <u>dreaming</u> about your success and <u>work</u> for it.

Learn to Excel through Ability

What do Joe Montana, Beverly Sills, Andrew Wyeth, Chris Evert, Van Cliburn, and Jonas Salk have in common, beyond being Americans of the Twentieth Century? All of them are (or were) better than almost anyone else at their chosen callings, and all (start taking notes at this point) subjugated their personalities and emotions to their intellect and talents. People who truly excel find little need to play the *hey-look-at-me!* game. They don't dye their hair garish colors. They don't wear rings in their noses. They don't tattoo their bodies. They are content with their own excellence, and they let that excellence do the talking.

Outlandish, flamboyant people are invariably those who are starved for attention and believe success is measured by how much other people admire them. They always lack either the intelligence or the talent to be noted for what they do and usually take a back seat to others who are better at their profession than they are. Since they can't make it to the top on their own merits, they try to steal the spotlight by dressing like clowns, wearing tons of jewelry or makeup, and saying things that are supposed to be clever or shocking. But more often than not they're just loud and undeniably stupid. You will find greater happiness through sincerity, hard work, attention to detail, diligent study, and good manners than you ever will by being loud, obnoxious, and irreverent.

Rule #7: If you want to be noticed, do it by being better at what you do than anyone else.

Accept Your Limits And Your Strengths

Few people are more detrimental to human progress than the meddlers. It seems to be a universal human weakness that someone who gains even minimal acclaim in one field feels compelled to spill over into areas where he or she is unskilled. Many of you will be able to relate this problem to the Peter Principle, made famous by Lawrence Peter: "In a hierarchically structured administration, people tend to be promoted up to their level of incompetence." However, I like to generalize this concept with the Smith Maxim:

*In any human endeavor, the final decision will be made
by the person who is least qualified to make it.*

Let's say, for example, that a man makes a fortune in real estate or insurance, then indulges a lifelong wish and buys a professional baseball franchise. He owns the team, but was it his success and talent that brought him to the elevated status of team owner? No. It was just his money. It is inevitable that within a month he will be questioning the decisions made by team managers and players and no more than two months until he is positioning the outfield. He knows, after all, how to be successful, so why shouldn't he be able to make the team successful, too?

What our hypothetical man is doing is *meddling* in a field he knows nothing about. The actor wants to sing. The singer wants to direct. The director probably wants to tap dance up and down the Capitol Building steps. When this compulsion is accompanied by money and authority, there is no one to stop the sickness, and we commonly wind up with an inevitable, substandard performance.

Our society likes to teach us that if we just chant the words, "I know I can, I know I can!" long enough, then we will inevitably succeed. In reality, there really are things we cannot do or that will not happen no matter how much chanting we do.

Knowing what you cannot do is a trait as desirable as knowing what you can do. There is nothing wrong with the word *can't* (any more than with the word No). An intelligent person is aware of what he cannot do and leaves those areas to people who are good at them. Multitalented people are almost always fairly good at one thing and mediocre in all the rest. I don't think that a real triple-threat halfback ever lived, and I have grave doubts about anyone with a hyphenated occupation. For example, there is an entire cottage industry of editors and ghost writers whose primary function is to straighten out the mess left by celebrities who think they can write.

It's OK to Say No!

It is important to understand that collectively speaking, few people ever excel at anything. But through study and hard work, you can reach a plateau of excellence. And once you reach that plateau you can rejoice, then strive to be even better. Don't push into areas where you have no business being. Accept the fact that somebody is always going to be better than you at something. Carl Sandburg understood this, and so do Lou Holtz and Zubin Mehta.

Rule #8: Be content with what you're good at and leave the rest to someone else.

Spend Less than You Earn

This is a law of economics that is so simple you can only wonder at why it's broken so often. The great scourge of modern existence is debt—overwhelming, suffocating, unrelenting debt. It is a leading cause of divorce, suicide, and mental disorder. The only way to avoid it is through self-discipline. Two contrasting examples of this situation come to mind: a lady named Molly, and a couple, Iris and Ralph.

Molly is someone we knew when her son was a classmate with our son at a private school in Los Angeles. Molly wanted the best education obtainable for her boy, but couldn't afford the tuition. Her husband saw nothing wrong with public school and was no help at all. Rather than plunge into a great and lasting debt to accomplish her purpose, she volunteered to drive a school bus in exchange for the tuition money, which she did for twelve years, and was present to see him graduate from high school.

The saga of Iris and Ralph, on the other hand, was different. They were two people I knew slightly (but never wanted the relationship to grow). They found themselves in debt up to their eyeballs and were making no attempt to alter the situation. They had driven all credit card accounts over the top and were about to lose their home when an interested relative put them into the hands of a financial counselor. The man called all of their creditors, arranged for loan extensions, and put them on a reasonable financial footing. Having dodged the bullet, Ralph gained renewed vigor and was heard to say, "Now that we have things under control, we can take that trip to Paris." They went, charging the whole thing!

Rule #9: *If you can't afford it, don't buy it.*

Always Let Reason Overrule Emotion

Never make a major decision based on emotion. This includes marriage, buying a house or a car, or accepting a transfer to another city. Emotions need to be let out and aired occasionally (they're useful when you need to express yourself), but it's the intellect that must rule your life.

A wise axiom encourages you to "Think Before You Leap!" An enormous amount of unhappiness can be avoided if you just take the time to think ahead. If you know that A leads to B, and that B will probably lead to C, and if C is something that makes you unhappy, then avoid *A.*

Another aspect of this problem is the fact that those who can't learn from history are doomed to repeat it. In other words, if something didn't work yesterday, it probably won't work today. If the same thing has repeatedly gotten you into trouble, it will get you into trouble again.

Our emotions can cause us to repeat the same silly mistake over and over in the hope that *this time* the results will be different—*this time* we'll succeed. Why can outside observers point out the flaw in this type of thinking so easily? Because they're not emotionally tied to it. They can use their intellect and be objective!

Rule #10: *Take the time to think about your choices before you make a decision.*

Avoid "In" Things and "In" People

To the teenagers of the world, there is probably nothing more important than being *in:* hanging out with the right people, saying all kinds of hip things, and doing the cool things that seem important to minds just beginning to ripen. Fortunately, most people outgrow this by their early twenties—it's called *growing up.* But a few airheads carry this mentality all the way through to senility. I call it the *Beverly Hills Disease,* and it can easily be identified in the case of middle-aged men and women who actually care about being seen in the right restaurants, shopping in the right stores, and vacationing in places frequented by the "trendsetters."

People who follow fads are rarely wealthy or successful on their own. They're usually blowing the hard-earned money they received from an inheritance. Following them will cause you to lose your money, too. It will also restrict your friendships and associates to people who generally haven't a clue about how to succeed by themselves. If you're to get anywhere in this life, the day must come when you turn your back on the trendsetters and start leading your own life. Stand tall, build your talents, work hard, and people will start looking up to *you.*

Rule #11: Learn to live like an adult. Remember what the Bible teaches: "When I was a child, I spake as a child, I understood as a child, I thought as a child: but when I became a man [or woman], I put away childish things."

Live Defensively

In fencing, the act of defending yourself against a thrust is called a *parry.* Learn to parry the thrusts of life at an early age. Remember that the world is populated with people who exist by keeping others permanently pinned against the wall. The answer is to stay away from the wall and out of the corners of life. Have your excuses ready in advance and become proficient at evasion. Don't be trapped into something that you don't want to do.

Be especially wary of the "bait-and-switch" attack which is used by people who first find out that you're available and then spring the trap. These people may begin a conversation with something like, "What are you doing Saturday night?" and follow up your, "Not much," reply by automatically including you in their plans. When you see this thrust, parry immediately with concrete plans of your own—"My wife and I have dinner reservations," or "An old friend is in town and I've invited him over for dinner and a movie." The answer to the thrusts of life is to be prepared for every eventuality—to live defensively.

Now, I know that some say the best defense is a good offense, but I don't think this is always true. A good offense in life would translate to always being unavailable, such as living as a hermit in a distant forest, and that's no solution. In my opinion the best defense is a strong, well-planned web of protection that will withstand attack. The ideal solution would be to hire a social secretary who screens everything and keeps the gophers from your roses. Most of us can't afford this, however, and are left to our own devices. We need imagination, foresight, and determination that we aren't going to be roped into anything we don't want to do.

Rule #12: *Be prepared to say "No" to unwanted incursions into your life.*

Go to College if at All Possible

Most of the people who "couldn't" go to college or who "didn't have the opportunity" are stretching the truth more than a little. There are rare cases in which a young person finishes high school, then needs to go to work to support his ailing parents or a large number of younger siblings. But even that is becoming a thing of the past. With all of the programs available to help young people further their educations, most people without a college education simply didn't want to go. It was too much work, and the prospect of getting a job and buying a car seemed like a more attractive road to follow. Later, when faced with the prospects of lower paying jobs and social limitations, they could always moan that "they didn't have the opportunity," and this would cover a lot of laziness.

Universities do much more than just dispense knowledge. They also teach discipline and responsibility and provide intellectual resources. Many high school graduates complain that the college grads get all the breaks in hiring ("I know as much as that guy knows"), but remember that the interviewer has little to go on beyond a quick conversation and a resume. A college degree demonstrates to the interviewer that the applicant had the intestinal fortitude to stay in school for at least four years, the intelligence to do the required work, and the organizational ability necessary to prioritize all of the responsibilities in life so that he or she could achieve a goal—the college degree. Anyone can quit, and many people do. But the ones who make it all the way have something to enter on the plus side of an employer's ledger.

It is also an interesting and quite valid consideration that college is the first thing a person does in life that isn't mandatory. No one can make this person study, much less pass courses, and anyone who is bent on flunking out will fail. People who elect to finish the difficult job of acquiring an education, however, show a notable bit of character at an early age.

Rule #13: *Go to college. Nothing in life is more valuable than your education.*

Accept the Word No as the Best Friend You'll Ever Have

Teaching yourself to say "No" is the most important of all my rules; therefore, I've saved it for last. Put in its simplest form, when you can say "No," you are in control of your own life.

You must take control if you are to succeed in life—and you aren't too young to start. You can listen to the myths, the half-truths, and the general nonsense of the sunshine philosophers, or you can put your brain into gear and start moving forward on the solid impetus of your intellect. Learn to think things through. Learn to say "No" to things that make you unhappy. There is nothing better I can tell you.

Rule #14: *Learn to say "No."*

RECAP OF SMITH'S SIMPLE RULES TO LIVE BY

1. Stop complaining in no-win situations and move on to something productive.
2a. (For the ladies): date the jocks if you want, but marry the nerds
2b. (For the men): date the airheads if you must, but marry the girls who can help you succeed in life.
3. Act responsibly; either commit to marriage or commit to being single.
4. Learn quickly from the people who already have the answers.
5. Don't take foolish risks.
6. Avoid the Positive Thinking mentality.
7. If you want to be noticed, do it by being better at what you do than anyone else.
8. Be content with what you're good at and leave the rest to someone else.
9. If you can't afford it, don't buy it.
10. Take the time to think about your choices before you make a decision.
11. Learn to live like an adult.
12. Be prepared to say "No" to unwanted incursions into your life.
13. Go to college. Nothing in life is more valuable than your education.
14. Learn to say "No" to things that make you unhappy.

Learn to Write Off Unhappiness

> You owe nothing to anyone who
> owes nothing to you.

In the last chapter I introduced a list of rules we can teach our children that if followed, could help them lead happier lives. However, the rest of us need to do a little *unlearning*—a process that inevitably comes with emotional "baggage," baggage that we need to eliminate from our lives.

Most of us are taught from day one that selfishness is wrong and putting someone else's needs ahead of ours is right. But at the risk of angering Christians around the world, let me propose a different viewpoint.

If you study the Bible closely, you'll find that it does not actually condemn selfishness. What it teaches is that generosity to those in need is good behavior; going the extra mile to help a brother is good behavior; tolerance and patience are also good behaviors. But if Christ taught us anything, He taught us the need to protect ourselves from evil: from those who would harm us or rob us of our happiness.

This, I believe, is where many parents falter. Rather than teaching their children how to serve their own needs first and serve others second, they teach them that they should be willing to sacrifice everything—including their own happiness—to help every beggar on the street, deserving or not.

What my viewpoint forces adults to do is unlearn the belief that they are nothing and others are everything, and teach them to understand and respect their own needs. This can be a very painful experience, but the rewards are greater than anyone can imagine. What we need to do is write off the things that make us unhappy—including people if necessary.

Let me give you an example. I knew a woman named Leslie several years ago when we worked together in Los Angeles. She was divorced and the mother of two teenage daughters. Leslie married a man who also worked with us, and everyone agreed that it was a very good match. However, it was the termination of her first marriage that provides a lesson for anyone who is willing to listen.

Her first husband—the father of her children—was a drunk, and Leslie had put up with his drinking for years. She suffered through his brief periods on the wagon, his promises never to drink again, and the great, gut-wrenching disappointments when he would come home late and pass out on the bed—always hoping the next time would be different.

Then one night she wised up, and her first husband lost his wife and his two children, all while he was unconscious; that's a terrible price to pay for one more drink. Leslie, however, had experienced a revelation—the kind that happens so rarely in one's lifetime that it must be cherished when it occurs.

As she tells it, there was no emotion involved. During a time of maximum stress she made a cold, rational decision, because that decision had to be made for her protection and the protection of her children. She looked at the disgusting lump lying across the foot of the bed and simply knew that her marriage was over.

The immediate effect of this revelation and the powerful decision that Leslie made was that she stopped caring if her first husband went on drinking or not. In her mind, she saw two choices: continue with a dead-end life, hoping for something that was never going to happen, or start over.

What Leslie did was write him off. *His problem was no longer her problem*—it was no longer something she had to share. She got her children out of bed, packed their bags, and moved that night—effectively separating herself from a problem that never should have been hers in the first place. Instead, she turned in a direction that would provide more happiness for both herself and her children.

Leslie explained that the husband made some impassioned phone calls over the next few weeks, promising all kinds of personal rebirth if she would only take him back. To her credit, she refused. The decision had been made and it was irrevocable. She wrote him off like a bad debt.

I have said repeatedly in these pages that personal problems must be solved intellectually, not emotionally—and this is exactly what Leslie did. Indeed, it was what she had to do. In a moment of rare insight, she recognized her husband as a source of unending misery—so she cut the man out of her life and relieved herself of a lot of emotional baggage.

This isn't to say that Leslie stopped caring for her first husband as a person; I'm sure she still wishes he'd stop drinking. But she stopped caring about him as a wife. Caregivers have responsibilities, but what those responsibilities are depends on the role the caregiver plays in someone's life. As long as Leslie cared about the drunk on her bed as a wife, she couldn't relinquish her emotional ties. The moment she changed her outlook from caring wife to caring stranger on the street, she was able to dump him in the gutter and move on with her life.

I firmly believe that this is the way many of our problems must be met and solved. If a person causes nothing but misery for others, the only solution is the write-off. You can become part of someone else's perennial problem and suffer from things you did not cause, or you can distance yourself from the whole mess and start to live your own life.

As I speak with people, I find that the resistance to this solution is always emotional. "I just can't turn my back. After all, this is my [mother, father, sister, brother, son, daughter, old friend, second cousin (take your pick)]." Emotions are useful for identifying problems, but they're useless for fixing them. People with perennial problems, for example, are going to bring you into the middle of their self-made bag of misery, and you will stay there as long as emotion rules your life.

A Little Selfishness Goes a Long Way

As I mentioned, we are taught as children that we must never be selfish. This is fine if we're talking about tinker toys, dolls, or electric trains. When it comes to living, however, we sometimes need to be selfish to survive (and certainly to be happy).

I spoke with a lady shortly after the publication of my book, *How to Cure Yourself of Positive Thinking,* and she told me that her 28-year-old daughter had brought her nothing but grief for the previous 12 years. The girl had been a drug user and was expelled from high school. She had been arrested several times, had lived with men who physically abused her, had shoplifted, and had generally made one stupid, destructive decision after another for years. The mother was involved because the daughter periodically came home for a little R&R before the next series of misadventures. The mother repeated the old hand wringing refrain of, "Where did I go wrong?"—which solved nothing.

My advice to her (as it is to *all* people in her shoes) was to "drive the snakes from the garden." When one person brings nothing but misery into the life of another, then that person simply has to go. In effect, it is an act of divorce. Remember that we're *not* talking about the traditional helping hand. Most of us are quite willing to help family and friends with unforeseen difficulties and it's right that we should; but what we're dealing with here is the *chronic* problem case—someone who is, always has been, and always will be a problem to other people. You don't need this person in your life even if this person is a son or a daughter. No one does. And you have to muster the strength to do something about it.

Playing on the Same Playing Field

Remember that no game can be played by two sets of rules. The person who is causing the problem is being *completely selfish*, caring nothing about the feelings or welfare of the people who are being dragged into his or her mess. It would seem only reasonable to assume that the other players in the game should be allowed to be selfish as well; this is the nature of protecting yourself from those who would do you harm. You have the right to ask a favor of me, and I have the right to refuse. These rules should make sense to everyone involved.

Sometimes, the rationale for the offending person's actions is "sickness," which is the all-purpose excuse for any kind of anti-social behavior. We are supposed to accept the reprehensible assertion that nasty, ill-mannered, rude, and generally offensive people are "sick," and that we are obliged to put up with them because they can't help themselves. Rubbish! When these people have enough doors slammed in their faces and stop receiving handouts from family, friends, government, and the psychiatric community in general, they might just find a "cure" *all by themselves.*

✦ ✦ ✦

Let me pause for a moment and note that the selfishness I advocate is reactive in nature. I am not saying that you should cut the biggest piece of pie for yourself, or refuse to accept reasonable family and social obligations. I'm not even suggesting that you avoid helping someone who's out of work. What I am suggesting is that intelligent, constructive selfishness is a wall that protects a person from unwanted and undeserved incursions. Chronic, self-made, and never-ending problems belong to the creator of those problems, and they should not be shared. You are under no obligation to help people who make no effort to help themselves. If you learn nothing else in your journey through life, learn this.

Note that I have used the word *reactive;* you do not initiate the selfishness, but employ it only as a reaction to those who make unreasonable demands on you. It is a defensive weapon, a means of protecting yourself from evil, *and it should only be used in this way*. When it is used, however, use both barrels.

✦ ✦ ✦

Getting back to the matter of "sickness," we should see this for what it is. *Sickness* refers to the imposition of an external force that creates an abnormal condition. When applied to the body, *sickness* refers to the effects of bacteria, viruses, infection, etc., that invade the body and pull it away from the healthy norm.

The difficulty with Problem Perennials claiming to be sick is that they are depending on the vague and usually subjective definition of *mental* illness. I wholeheartedly agree that bacteria, viruses, infections, chemicals, and other external forces can invade the brain and have an effect on the mind. I also agree that in some cases, this is unavoidable and requires the generous help of individuals or society. My problem is when people define mental illness outside of the context of *choice*.

People *choose* to take drugs. Yes, the drug can and does become addictive, but that's not a sickness, that's the consequence of a *bad choice*. When a person breaks into a house and steals, it's a bad choice. When a person uses foul language in public, it's a bad choice. When a man rapes, it's a bad choice.

Frankly, this sickness routine makes me a little, well . . . *sick*. People who drink too much like to think they have a disease, which gets them around the problem of being responsible for their choices. (To quote the old Flip Wilson line, "The Devil made me do it.") People who steal from stores, run up huge debts on their credit cards, neglect their families, refuse to work, shoot illegal drugs into their veins, even those who eat too much are currently said to be suffering from illness and therefore should not be censured for their actions. I sometimes wonder if psychiatrists don't have enough to do. (I suspect they need to justify their existence—which can't be done unless someone is *sick*.)

What really burns me up is the results of all this nonsense. Honest, hardworking people are drained of time and resources and their blood pressure is raised by people who use the claim of sickness to avoid responsibility. I would like to play by the same rules, so I want to claim sickness (I'm sick of them) and avoid any and all responsibility they think I should have toward them. Every honest, hardworking person in our country should have this privilege.

But there's a better way! Give the supposedly sick people in your life a firm and resounding, "No!" and invite them in no uncertain terms to get out of your life.

Let the Emotional Burden Go

The only way to instill an attitude of "constructive selfishness" into our psyche is first to teach ourselves to let our emotional burdens go. Most of the time, emotional burdens take the form of an implicit obligation such as, "He's your son, you owe it to him to let him come home." People who live with perpetual obligations to others are actually *slaves*. They have been robbed of the control they should have over their lives and spend their lives reacting to the demanding and unreasonable behavior of someone else. As hard as it may be for those of you who suffer from this malady, this must change.

Remember, it's the moochers, the dumpers, the Problem Perennials who perpetuate the obligation game and keep the you-owe-me nonsense alive. And why shouldn't they, as long as it works? No one ever seems to turn the situation around and ask what these people owe anyone else.

The entire thing has been reduced to a single formula by my friend, the Sage of Bakersfield, who advances the *Two-Mess Rule* as a guide for both the dumpers and the dumpees. Simply put, the rule states that one person will bail another person out of a mess only twice in a lifetime. That's all. Two times and you're through. No more credit. And there's no greater relief from an emotional burden than knowing that it won't go on forever.

Here's an example. The Sage told me that he once let an ever-needy cousin be evicted from his home because the cousin had used up his supply of "bail-outs." The first occasion occurred in the middle of the night when the Sage towed his cousin's car from a ditch. On the second occasion, the Sage put up bail money to get his cousin out of jail. That was it. The man had used his two chances and the Sage was through with him. The cousin never spoke to the Sage again, of course, but the Sage opined that losing this person's friendship was like losing a canker sore—it was gone, with no regrets.

The Two-Mess Rule may sound harsh, but it's actually a very good rule. There is nothing magic about the number, however, and you could determine the number to be greater or smaller, depending on the degree of your largesse. Choose the number of times you are willing to shoulder the burden of someone else's self-made pain and after that number is reached, rid yourself of the burdens imposed by this individual. The important thing is that there should be a limit placed on a Problem Perennial's demands. There must be a time when the saturation point is reached and someone says, *enough!* After you've done it once, it's such a good feeling that you'll want to do it again.

Protecting Yourself Is Not a Sin

When employed sensibly and responsibly, selfishness can be a desirable thing indeed. I think this idea has a definite correlation with the writings of the great German philosopher Immanuel Kant. It was Kant who formulated the Categorical Imperative:

Act as if the maxim of your action were to become through your will a general natural law.

Kant's imperative is an ethical principle that is applicable to our daily conduct, and it most certainly can be applied to everything that has been discussed in this chapter. It's actually a spin-off from the Golden Rule that various people have expressed in different ways, including the contemporary, "What goes around comes around," and that grand old favorite of the U.S. Navy, "Shape up, or ship out!"

Kant is saying that we should act at all times as though we would want our actions to become an acknowledged universal law. In the case of our ability to understand our strengths and weaknesses, (and the strengths and weaknesses of others) and our ability to identify people whom we cannot help (or, better said, those who *will* not be helped) and should be written off, I ask, do we want this practice to become a "universal law" in our day-to-day lives? I suggest that we do, as it is a sure path to happiness. It is only fitting, then, that the personal write-off becomes the natural way of things. If this practice actually did come to pass, then after repeated offenses:

- The drunk and the drug abuser would either find professional help and truly change, or face the consequences of their actions by themselves—never burdening anyone again.
- Bad check artists would go to jail. No one would show up to cover the loss.
- People who spend the rent money at the track would be evicted.
- Anyone running from the police or from bill collectors would be given no place to hide.
- The deadbeat who needs immediate cash to get out of a self-made mess would be thrown right back into that mess.
- Philandering spouses would not get back inside the door.
- The habitual liar would be exposed and discredited.

At first blush this may sound harsh, but it isn't. What I've described is nothing more than the consequences of bad choices! Exempting those people who dedicate their lives to helping others, no one should be forced to bear the burden of another person's bad choices. This isn't being selfish—it's being sane.

Think about it. Would the world be any worse off today if any of this happened? I think not. In fact, we might have a much better society (which is a good segue to my next chapter.) We need these people like we need ringworm, and I see no point in prolonging a situation that isn't going to end until the exploited party ends it. You can bet on the fact that the people who live off the body heat of productive society certainly won't call a halt to their bad behavior by themselves.

> An invader either stays or is driven out; he never leaves voluntarily.

The happiest people in the world are those who understand selfishness—the need to protect themselves from evil and exploitation—and who realize that it has a worthwhile place in human existence. These people put responsible limits on their charity, and they know exactly how far those limits will bend before the bending even starts. They truly control those aspects of their lives that they can and should control, for without that control there can be no happiness.

In summary, when we think of selfishness, let us see it in terms of self-interest rather than self-indulgence. It's not a matter of keeping all of the toys, but rather of setting limits so that a certain part of our existence is not open to exploitation. Think of it as a sort of "Monroe Doctrine" for the soul. We should say to the world, "Enjoy me for who and what I am, not for what I can do for you."

It seems like a reasonable thing to ask.

Saying "NO" as a Society

> The professional criminal has voluntarily chosen his profession. All that society asks of him is that he stop doing what he is doing, and this doesn't seem to be an unreasonable request. Obeying the law requires no talent and no training. Anyone can do it.

The above quote originally appeared in an article I wrote for *The Freeman* (ISSN 0016-0652) and was picked up by *Reader's Digest* in its November 1991 issue. The point is found in the last sentence: "Anyone can do it."

Obeying the law is not an impossible, or even a difficult, request. Those who choose not to adhere to the rules of a civilized society do so of their own volition; therefore, society is free to assume that they are willing to pay the price.

In all previous chapters we have been talking about the word No as it applies to the individual, but communities and societies can also say "No" when addressing social or other community problems. We all should remember that communities and societies are nothing more than a group of individuals with common interests—and when those common interests are violated, the individuals rise up in unity to say "No." (A sterling example is the American Revolution.)

In this and the subsequent chapter, I will address two specific issues that impact a community: crime and business. This chapter will deal specifically with the problem of crime—and the only answer to this problem that makes any sense to me is to build bigger jails. If two-thirds of the population must keep the other one-third locked up to protect itself, then so be it.

Dealing with the Root of Crime

I can recall adult conversations from my earliest childhood in which everyone agreed that we had to "deal with the root of crime." This was always spoken in a tone of finality, as though someone had just solved a problem. People were probably nodding in somber agreement with this observation for many generations before I came along, but unfortunately, no one has even come close to finding this mysterious "root." No one has found a universal crime *disease* or a crime *gene* (though many have tried to justify crime through upbringing or particular lifestyles). As a society, we can continue to add our own assent to this tidy bit of bumper-sticker philosophy, but it won't accomplish anything because it's nothing more than an observation of a social need.

The primary problem with the issue of crime is that there is no single yardstick by which the tendency to commit crime can be measured. People will choose to become involved in criminal activity for as many reasons as there are people on the earth. My liberal friends assure me that poverty is the root of crime and that a massive slum clearance and government handout programs will have everyone loving his neighbor and joining hands in song. I say hogwash! If we accept this premise, then we must also accept the belief that all rich people are innately pure of heart and the upper middle-class is at least partially angelic. I just haven't found this to be true.

Rich people rob, rape, and kill, and poor people often rise to become public benefactors. White, yellow, red, and black people all commit crimes. Protestants, Catholics, Jews, Moslems, and Buddhists break the law every day. Children from good homes grow up to become drug pushers and axe murderers. We know *why* people commit crimes (greed, lust, anger, etc.), but we don't have a magic pill that makes the tendencies go away or a magic machine that can change the way people think and feel. So we can do nothing more than punish people once they prove they will not abide by the rules of a civilized society.

From most people's point of view, dealing with the root of crime is not the process of finding the crime *gene*—it's the task of using the tools at hand to stop the perpetrators of crime from harming society further.

Using the Tools at Hand

To illustrate the idea of using the tools that we have, let's examine the medical profession. Physicians of earlier times are considered to have been quite primitive (just as today's medicine will be seen as something from the Stone Age only 100 years from now). My great grandfather, who fought with a Minnesota regiment in the Civil War, caught a bullet in his leg and was carted off to a barn where a waiting surgeon amputated the limb with a saw. It was a ghastly experience, but it undoubtedly saved his life. He lived to see his eightieth birthday.

No one can fault the physicians of any era—or the firemen, aviators, sea captains, engineers, and those in other professions—for using the knowledge and tools available to them to do their jobs. Do we fault the designers of the Tacoma Narrows Bridge for its collapse? At the time of its design and construction, this bridge was hailed as revolutionary—a creation of grace and beauty that represented the highest achievement of the time-tested tenets of civil engineering—and then it collapsed. The engineers of the day did the best they could with the tools they had. We do not fault them for the abrupt education we all received when the bridge failed, but we do expect them to learn from such catastrophes—and they did.

By this same logic, we can't fault the people of law enforcement for using the only time-tested tool available to them to curb crime: incarceration. As I said before, we have no magic pills or brainwashing machines. All we can do is separate the incorrigible members of society from the rest of us, and hope they'll get the message. And if they don't, then we'll continue to separate them.

There are some people who argue that prisons do not rehabilitate. I agree—but I hasten to add a heartfelt, "So what?" to my response. In only the most rare and compassionate of circumstances do the victims of crime desire the rehabilitation of their assailants. Generally, these victims want two things: compensation, and *never to be hurt again*. Courts of law address the victim's first want—prisons address the second.

Demanding Personal Responsibility

Prisons do not rehabilitate; people rehabilitate. The message society sends to criminals must be loud and clear: if you don't want to be locked away, then don't break the law—*it's your choice*.

Adherents of prison rehabilitation programs are quick to point out that society is not benefited if the prisoner is not rehabilitated. I vehemently disagree with this statement. Though I agree that a rehabilitated criminal could benefit society, I must point out that society also benefits while the lawbreaker is in prison. Every rapist behind bars spares at least one woman from being raped. Jailed bank robbers don't rob banks, and imprisoning a murderer guarantees that some innocent person will live to see another dawn. From my point of view as a member of civilized society, I demand but one thing from inmates: choose to live by the rules, or stay in jail.

There are many in our country who choose to view prisons as a measure of our society's failure—that we are unable to "raise" people of good repute. I disagree completely because I believe strongly in *personal* responsibility. It isn't society's responsibility to make sure you are a good person, it's yours. Prisons are therefore an asset to every society. It really is a simple matter. If the person who would otherwise burglarize your house is already in prison, you come out a winner in the deal.

Are Prisons Unfair to the Poor?

There are pundits among us who would have us believe that prisons represent a repressive class system. We have all yawned to the old refrain that the rich and powerful never go to jail, that only the poor are ever convicted. This is absurd. Examples like Nathan Leopold, Richard Loeb, Leona Helmsley, and Martha Stewart prove that rich people who break the law go to jail.

When it was announced that F. Lee Bailey was going to defend Patricia Hearst, the pundits chanted in a collective chorus that she would never spend a day in jail. No one could beat that Hearst–Bailey combination. Yet she *was* found guilty, and she *did* spend time behind bars.

Leopold and Loeb were represented by famed defense attorney Clarence Darrow. And Leona Helmsley's and Martha Stewart's attorneys weren't exactly bargain-basement barristers either. But they all lost their bid for freedom, and they all spent their time in jail.

Many other rich and powerful people can be added to our list of examples, including Walter Wanger, Albert B. Fall, Charles Forbes, Bobby Baker, and William Marcy Tweed. Although it's true that the best attorneys tend to be the most expensive, it is also true that the courts do not recognize an elite class that is above the law. As a veteran of four separate tours of jury duty and a member of at least a dozen panels, I've *never* heard a juror suggest that the defendant appeared to be rich so the jury had better vote for acquittal. Never, in fact, have I encountered more conscientious and fair-minded individuals than the average American who is closeted in a jury room trying to deliver a verdict. These men and women are not dazzled by slick lawyers, and they are not impressed with anyone's income or social standing.

Our prisons are full of criminals—some rich, some poor, some white, some black, some English speaking, some not, some in good health, and some not. Although individuals involved in the legal system will occasionally be influenced by prejudice and intolerance, the legal system of our society per se will not. Break the law and you'll go to jail—and society is better for it.

Solve Today's Problems Today

What the *get-to-the-root-of-crime* people never seem to understand is that crime is an *immediate* problem. If they want to continue hunting for the elusive root, let them proceed, but not at the expense of the viable solution we have today. Until we find a way to prevent individuals from becoming criminals and harming innocent people, the only sensible plan of action is to put the criminal where he cannot do any additional damage: behind bars.

It was California's ex-governor, Jerry "Moonbeam" Brown, who said, "Prisons don't rehabilitate, they don't punish, they don't protect, so what in hell do they do?" By merely asking such a question, the speaker reveals the incredible naiveté of the anti-prison crowd. The answer to his question—"What in hell do they do?"— is as simple as it is apparent to the logical mind. Prisons separate the bad guys from the good guys. This is all they do, and they do it very well. All of the handwringers who go around deploring the lack of rehabilitation during a prison term have lost sight of the basic purpose of prisons, which is to put a wall between the perpetrators of crime and their victims, just as a zoo puts a wall between the lions and the zebras. If a prisoner is interested in rehabilitation, we can all wish him success (I'll be the first to do so); but if not, another cell is waiting.

> Anyone who wants to be a civilized human being has but to stop being a monster.

Capital Punishment is a Permanent Prison

In the area of capital punishment we once again see the handwringers at work, deploring the perceived "cruelty" of it all and fighting to gain lighter sentences for the most vicious predators on the face of this planet. Almost as naïve as Jerry Brown's curiosity about the value of prisons are some of the statements made by that vociferous band of people who oppose capital punishment. Here are a few of my favorites:

1. Execution will not bring the victim back. Life without parole accomplishes the same goal.
2. Capital punishment is not a deterrent to crime.
3. Televising executions will convince people never to execute a person again.
4. Capital punishment dehumanizes a society.

Let's look at each of these illogical arguments in turn.

Execution will not bring the victim back. This is absolutely true—but who ever said that it would? Imprisonment won't bring the victim back either, nor will a sharp reprimand or requiring the murderer to write, "I will not kill people," on a blackboard 100 times. Execution has nothing to do with bringing dead people back to life. It is a punishment—the *consequence* of *taking a* human life, which is by far the worst crime a human being can commit.

Life without parole will accomplish the same goal. There is no such thing as imprisonment without the possibility of parole. As long as a heart beats in the chest of a murderer, *someone* will be working night and day to put him back on the street. A law can be rescinded as easily as it can be made, and we have no guarantees whatsoever that the worst of humankind will not be turned loose to walk someday among the best of us. However, execution settles the matter permanently. It is the only "permanent prison."

Capital punishment is not a deterrent to crime. Statistics have been used by both pro-capital punishment and anti-capital punishment camps to prove that execution is (or is not) a deterrent. The two sides can drag out the same numbers and debate the issue into eternity with very little ever being settled. There is, however, another argument that is rarely made, one that is very difficult to counter: anyone who walks the last mile in death row is being thoroughly deterred. We can guarantee—absolutely and with certainty—that *this person* will not kill again. People with attractive, dark-haired daughters have known since January of 1989 that Ted Bundy will never again lurk behind the shrubbery.

Televising executions will convince people never to execute a person again. If the gladiatorial games of yesteryear and the overly violent movies and video games we enjoy today aren't enough to disprove this ridiculous assertion, then let's consider the issue of *fairness*. The world is full of people who want their way (and only their way), and they'll fight to keep others from seeing the other side of the coin. So if we decide to televise the horrible experience of an execution simply to prove that it should not be allowed (better known as *trial by media*), then it seems only reasonable to precede it with a reenactment of the horrible crime as well—as an explanation of why the execution is necessary. Show the killer as he ties and binds his victims in a kneeling position, makes them beg for their lives, then shoots them one by one. Show him dragging a teenage girl into his van, torturing her, raping her repeatedly, and then strangling her and leaving her body in a drainage ditch to die. At this point, we are *ready* to witness the execution.

Capital punishment dehumanizes society. Capital punishment does not dehumanize; premeditated murder dehumanizes. Punishment for a dehumanizing crime is the mark of a civilized society.

The anti-capital punishment crowd (or, more accurately, the *anti-punishment* crowd) has missed the point of execution for as long as any logical person can remember. We are not talking deterrence here, and we are not talking rehabilitation. Premeditated murder is unique among all other transgressions. It is not comparable to kidnapping, armed robbery, or insider trading because it robs both the victim and society of something eminently valuable and irreplaceable. This crime must be intolerable to society, and under no circumstances can it be met with vacillation or indecision. Capital punishment is a social statement that says this crime is different from all other crimes and will be met with a unique and permanent punishment.

If execution does not deter other premeditated murders, or murders associated with rape, kidnapping, and other violent crimes, then so be it. It will still make this profound statement about our society: *we regard these crimes as inexcusable, and we will punish accordingly.*

Every time a door slams for the last time behind a convicted murderer, we reaffirm our status as a civilized society. To tolerate murder is to put ourselves back in dark caves, looking for a way to create fire and make axes out of rocks.

Strength and Maturity are needed to say "No!"

When we take a hard-line attitude against crime, we prove that we have matured enough as a civilization to astutely handle the word No. Our intellect and compassion may make us curious and lead us to seek explanations as to why a specific individual put his gun to the head of a storekeeper and demanded that person's earnings for the day—but we refuse to use such explanations to justify the assailant's *choice.* To borrow a phrase so eloquently used by Nancy Regan, "Just say no!" to anyone and everyone who would choose to hurt any member of our society, or who would choose to take from them anything that is rightfully theirs.

> Nothing is ever gained by tolerating the intolerable.

I find it difficult to understand the mind of a person who has more compassion for an assailant than the assailant's victim. The Biblical teaching that mercy should temper justice means punishment should fit the crime, not that criminals should enjoy rights and privileges denied to victims of a crime. And lest we forget, there are always more victims than one. Besides the person who suffers a specific injury, there are also parents, siblings, spouses, children, relatives, friends, neighbors, clients, vendors—even medical personnel—who all suffer when someone is victimized. Indeed, anyone who cannot feel safe walking the streets of our cities, day or night, is a victim. People who are forced to put bars over their windows are victims; people who must buy alarm systems for their homes, offices, and cars are victims; anyone who must chain up his or her bicycle while visiting a library is a victim; people who pay higher insurance premiums or higher taxes because of crime are victims—all people who must live in fear of the anti-social behavior of others are victims.

I once had the opportunity to visit a neighborhood in East Los Angeles where the residents lived in total fear of their surroundings. Bars protected the windows of their homes and many residents had (illegal) guns that were hidden, but accessible. They kept a minimum number of lights on at night ("We don't want to call attention to ourselves"), and they chained and double-bolted their doors. No one—I mean *no one*—left their houses at night for any reason. These people were prisoners when the sun went down and thugs became kings. The criminals owned the night and the police were essentially powerless.

It's a tragic situation when people have no choice but to live like this, and this is the case in many parts of every U.S. city. Decent people live in total fear, while comfortable, well-educated pundits argue that criminals should be treated with lighter sentences because the hoodlums' upbringing "made them do it." The honest and decent even suffer at the hands of activists who spend their time raising money for behaviorally spread diseases and for the welfare of people who only needed to keep their pants on to avoid their problems. If there is a social cause waiting for a white knight, it is definitely the plight of these honest, hard-working people who have been forced to build their own fortresses, and who pray to make it through each night.

> I would rather see ten people hungry, or twenty unemployed, than one who is afraid.

Strength and maturity are needed to say "No." We are taught as children (and rightly so) that we should be good, compassionate people, willing to help when we can—but we are rarely taught that a time comes when the consequences of a person's choices should be borne by that person alone. All civilized societies have as one of their tenets a willingness to help those who seek assistance. I would be the first to help honest people remove themselves from the welfare rolls and join the tax-paying workforce—but there comes a time when society must turn from its willingness to help to its need to protect, and that requires the strength and maturity to say "No!" to the people who cross the line.

✦ ✦ ✦

As stated in the quotation that opened this chapter, crime is a *voluntary* thing. The image of Jean Valjean stealing a loaf of bread to feed his family is not representative of crime in America. Today's criminal is what he is because he makes a conscious decision to flaunt the law and work in direct opposition to the rules of society. Those who want to sympathize with this kind of behavior have every right to do so, but I heartily wish they would stop blocking the path of those who are trying to solve the problem.

I have no sympathy whatsoever for the murderer, the bank robber, the drug dealer, the pimp, the car thief, or the burglar. And to those who would make it easier for these people and give them chance after chance after chance, I ask: What about the rest of us? Don't we count at all? We have only one shot at life, too, and we don't want to live it in fear, hiding behind barred windows with alarm systems and guns cocked and ready. The answer to the whole problem of crime is simple: support our police departments, build bigger jails, and fill them as often as necessary. For those who think this is a harsh attitude, remember that no one is forced to become a criminal. It is a self-made condition. For the most part, people go to prison because they've done something rotten. Staying out of the lockup is the easiest thing that anyone can do.

The simple truth is that we owe the criminal *nothing*—zero, zip, nada. He (or possibly she) brought his misfortune upon himself, and society is not to blame for the consequences of his chosen lifestyle. Crime is but one more problem that can be solved by the word No. The only difference in this case is that we all must say it together.

The Corporate Mentality

> Granting authority to a jackass is
> to turn dormant stupidity into
> dynamic incompetence.

We've discussed a lot of the problems that come into our lives when we avoid using the word No. We've also discussed how to learn to say "No" effectively. However, before I wrap up I want to discuss the one aspect of our lives that's a gray area—the corporate environment.

In most areas of our lives we either have complete control ("No, I don't want to see that movie!"), or no control at all ("An IRS auditor will arrive on Monday to review your taxes . . ."). In the case of holding a job in the corporate world, the amount of control we have varies and it's sometimes not clear how much we have at any given time. The reason for this is that business requires managers to manage. That's logical—until their personal wants or needs lead to mistakes. When managers make mistakes, they hurt a lot of people. When executives hide or ignore the mistakes made by their managers, they only worsen matters. So now that we've learned how to say "No," let me appeal to the managers of the world to learn how to accept the word *No*.

Positive Thinking Redux

As a longtime player in corporate America, I'm aware of the strong tie that exists between boardroom thought processes and Positive Thinking; the arcane philosophy that has played a large part in our lives for the past 50 years. (See chapter 1 for details). Its influence extends well beyond the walls of business. For example, I can state without the slightest hesitation that my upward mobility ended with the publication of my first book, *How to Cure Yourself of Positive Thinking.*

That book questioned this most hallowed tenet of corporate mentality, and the executives who had substantial control over my career saw the philosophy I advanced as something that struck at the vitals of the hierarchy (like telling Mrs. Vanderbilt that her daughter was going to marry a Baptist). At that time, I was at a loss to understand why any profit-making enterprise would object to a philosophy that stresses rational thought—I honestly felt that people just needed to know about the damage Positive Thinking was doing and the benefits of jettisoning it—but I soon learned that I had taken a potshot at a sacred cow.

To the uninitiated, it may seem odd that Big Business would cling so tightly to a principle of such questionable credibility. After all, the corporate mentality should be a hardheaded, dollars-and-cents kind of thing: plans should be made, processes should be reviewed, and aspects of the company that don't maximize profit or minimize expense should be done away with. You'd think that a well run business wouldn't receive half-baked ideas with much enthusiasm. The initiate quickly learns, however, that Big Business has swallowed the hook of Positive Thinking—and it shows no signs of letting go.

I believe the explanation for this otherwise inexplicable phenomenon rests in a chance occurrence of perfect timing. The Positive Thinking craze was unloaded on the American public during the 1950s as *enlightened* management. It's no surprise that this was coincident with a dramatic increase in the influence of business colleges on the business world—as if a person couldn't be successful in business unless they first received a degree. Under the terms of this new credo, the boss was supposed to "get closer" to the employees . . . to "care."

Without the help of any union, suggestion boxes began appearing on the walls of every factory and grievance committees were created to hear the complaints of the rank and file. Few business leaders were very serious about playing this game, but they all took a seat at the table. It was the fashionable thing to do in business at the time.

I believe that most business leaders of the day realized that the time was fast approaching when a boss could no longer say, "Do it because I said to do it!" Unions in the early 1900's had done much to move this along. Indeed, the natural evolution of a complex society (of which business is a microcosm) is to become more democratic—to permit people to have just enough control over their lives that they feel they're an active part of the whole. The tyrannical leadership styles of the 1800's were naturally doomed to evolve into a more robust and inevitably better way.

The tyrannical spirit, however, remained. Management was groping for a less offensive way of making its demands.

Then, suddenly, out of nowhere, came *Positive Thinking*, like the White Knight riding out of the royal forest. Now the boss could say, "I want a good, positive attitude," which translated into the same "do it" message, but went down a lot better, like medicine hidden in syrup.

For most of us, a *positive attitude* means we are willing to do the job right—to be creative and imaginative and use our skills to get the job done on time and under budget. In business parlance, a positive attitude means that people are willing to cooperate and not object to the work they are asked to do. The phrase is actually one of the most manipulative phrases ever introduced into the business world, and it is more often used to threaten menials than to draw excellence from the human soul. To object in the business world is to be *negative,* a no-no in both the Twentieth and Twenty-First Centuries.

It's OK to Say No!

The Effect on Employees

I entered corporate America directly out of college. At that time I was given some invaluable (though hard to believe) advice by an older employee. As it was spelled out to me, the company did not want to see "boat rockers" in its ranks. Such people were immediately marked with an indelible stamp and considered unpromotable. The basic idea, as I understood it, was that I would need to swallow my integrity during business hours and be a *team player* (a term, incidentally, that I still find rather nauseating to this day).

I soon learned that it was folly to stand up for a principle that no one wanted. It was a lot like saving a woman from an attacker, then seeing her walk off with him hand in hand while you lay bleeding on the sidewalk.

The message was clear: there is a time for courage and a time to mind one's own business, despite the cost to both my own integrity and to the company's bottom line.

I ended up participating in programs that cost twice as much as they should have because of mismanagement, and I slavishly followed the orders of some of the most incompetent managers I have ever encountered. I saw and tolerated waste and bungling that staggered the imagination. I saw boat rockers hung out to dry, with none of their peers having a kind word to say about them. They were dead in the water and quite alone, with the only thought ever expressed being, "They should have known better." I learned to keep my mouth shut and to view incompetence and inefficiency as necessary parts of living—much like toothaches and houseflies. And for my team-player services, I was rewarded with regular salary increases and promotions commensurate with my tenure.

But it all came to an abrupt end with the publication of my first book, even though the book never mentioned the company nor any manager by name. It did, however, question the holy icon of Positive Thinking, and for this I was given the "degradation shuffle," which is management's way of encouraging an employee in disfavor to leave voluntarily (easier on everyone, you know) and thus save the company a lot of trouble. I was shunted off to meaningless assignments in remote buildings, made to work for people who had once worked for me, and generally humiliated as often as they could get away with it. The weekly staff meeting is a good example of the way it was handled. I had attended a regular Friday morning meeting for about five years when suddenly the time and place of the meeting started changing every week, and I was never informed. The boss always "forgot" but would surely inform me the next time, which he never did. All of this simply because I felt a company should be more concerned with profit and efficiency than empty philosophy.

Fortunately, I started selling my book about that time, so I could ride out the situation with a light at the end of the tunnel. There were, however, so many other fellow employees dancing the degradation shuffle that it left me with a permanent bad taste in my mouth. One wonders how the orchestrators of this demeaning behavior can justify their actions (except with the lame excuse that they were being "team players").

Let me give you one more example. One friend of mine fell into disfavor and had his desk (literally) turned to face the wall. Then he was given no work to do. At first blush, this seems to be an ideal situation: to get paid for having no responsibilities. In reality, there is nothing even remotely pleasant about it. Generally, people enjoy being productive. As a species we want to work— to know that we have done something meaningful with our day. To sit at a desk and do *nothing* is incredibly boring. There was a rule about reading at one's desk or working crossword puzzles, etc., so this eliminated any kind of personal entertainment to help pass the time. He had no assignments in other parts of the plant, so there was no excuse to leave his desk, except to go to the men's room (and this time was carefully monitored). Excessive time away from the work station was a violation of company rules and grounds for dismissal, as were excessive absenteeism and non-business phone calls. Even prisons allow prisoners to do *something*. Doing *nothing* is the very epitome of cruel and unusual punishment. This man had the choice of staring at the wall or quitting. So, after about three weeks of the degradation shuffle, he quit.

Some of you might be asking, "Why didn't the company just fire him?" The answer is simple. If a big corporation has a justifiable reason to terminate an employee (e.g., excessive absenteeism, etc.), they owe the employee nothing. If the employee chooses to quit, they owe the employee nothing. But if the company doesn't have a justifiable reason to terminate an employee (i.e., he's only guilty of not being a team player), the company is responsible for severance pay. Get the picture?

The concept of the "team" is ostensibly harmless enough; after all, what objection could anyone have to the idea of everyone pulling together toward a common goal? The concept should work in business as it does on the playing field, right? Everybody contributes, team captains (i.e., management) use those contributions to make sensible decisions, and the game is won. However, when coupled with a philosophy like Positive Thinking, the "team" concept becomes counterproductive because it demands unquestioned support for all projects, good and bad.

We Should Say "No" to Bad Ideas!

The odds are that there was someone at Ford who thought the Edsel was a bad idea—that a market slot just did not exist for it. I'm sure someone at Lockheed fought the L1011 fiasco, and there were undoubtedly people at JC Penney and Sears who wanted to stay with the product line that had put them in the hearts and minds of the American consumer. All of these companies got into trouble with *bad ideas*, and these bad ideas were all endorsed by *team players* who weren't about to question anything.

There were probably team players who told Adolf Hitler that invading the Soviet Union was a good idea and positive thinkers who supported Pickett's Charge, and the Maginot Line. There is no idea so bad that it won't get support from *someone,* and if the upper levels of management back it, then you can go to the bank with a universal blessing.

My complaint is not that there can be no objection to cooperating in the completion of a project: if you're hired to do a job, you should honorably do the job. My complaint is that people should be allowed to uncover flaws. Indeed, they should be expected to! And who better to do that than the people who carry the spears into battle?

A good example of management marching off in the wrong direction occurs with the inevitable "economy wave" that rocks through most organizations on a regular basis. No one can object to the idea of cutting costs, but the economy wave is always implemented from the top down. Management makes arbitrary personnel cuts——often the best people (because they tend to have the highest salaries)——and merges departments that should never be merged. Why don't they work from the bottom up? Almost all workers know how their jobs could be done more efficiently, but no one ever asks them. Time and again I have seen muscle stripped from the bone while the fat remained—but objections were futile (agitators lose their jobs).

I could have saved my company a fortune without sacrificing a single job by cutting unnecessary overtime, streamlining the operation, and putting competent people (real managers) in charge. No one asked, however, and I couldn't volunteer my thoughts. I spent nearly twenty years as a valuable and trusted team player. I always adopted a positive attitude, even though I silently watched untold dollars being flushed down the toilet.

Let me give you a funny example: the Great Paper Clip Caper! Several years ago, one of the hourly employees in our company noticed a paper clip box on his desk. The label on the box claimed there were 100 clips inside. It was a new box. He knew that none of the clips had been removed. When he counted them, however, he found only 97 clips (please don't ask me *why* he felt compelled to count the clips). This intrepid employee then went to the supply cabinet, brought out other new boxes, and counted them all. There were fewer than 100 in each one. Following this, he spent the next few lunch hours counting every paper clip box in sight and he found that the company was being regularly shorted by a few clips per box. He made his findings known to his superiors, who passed the report on to the top echelons.

This discovery was well received because it was *safe*. It didn't tread on anyone's toes or highlight the incompetence of anyone's brother-in-law. The young man was commended and became the company's latest "White Knight." An article about him appeared in the company paper, along with the information that the paper clip supplier had been contacted and had agreed to make full restitution for the missing clips, along with assurances that all boxes henceforth would contain 100 clips. As a news item, it was treated like nothing less than the landing on D-Day.

The article appeared on a day when I was holding 17 people——on overtime pay, no less——waiting for one indecisive man to release the work that should have come to us that morning. The cost of the overtime was such that the company could have recovered the price of *every paper clip in its entire history* simply by replacing this klutz with someone who could make a decision. We burned money as though it were stacks of autumn leaves, all the while marching to glory with the Great Paper Clip Victory.

(As a side note, the indecisive manager brought me considerable wealth in a five-year feeding frenzy of unnecessary overtime. I put a new roof on my house, enlarged my patio, and installed an air-conditioning system, all because of one disorganized person who gummed up the works with amazing predictability. The company would not allow any criticism of this man, either. [It was a "sensitive issue."] So we all fattened up accordingly and kept the home contractors in business, except for the apartment dwellers who were content to use their overtime pay visiting foreign shores. Still, management was delighted to be compensated for at least 100 paper clips and to realize that conscientious employees were alert to available cost savings.)

As funny as these stories are, the sad truth is this sort of thing is occurring over and over again in business and in government. Industry in particular hurts itself immeasurably when it refuses to look at real problems and instead applauds *safe solutions to minor discrepancies*—as though they were the salvation of mankind. (I'm sure that those of you who work for large corporations have your own stories to tell of laughably ridiculous cost saving measures and insane managerial bungles.)

The Solution Requires Character

No one in management wants to be second-guessed by subordinates. By the same token, no one is infallible. If a subordinate has something to contribute, the world isn't going to end if someone in management listens. Change does not always have to originate at the top—and considering the pyramid shape of business hierarchy, positive change is far more likely to occur near the bottom.

The biggest problem facing American industry today stems directly from the conflict instigated by employers of the 1800's, who wanted to tyrannically control business operations, versus the opposing Twenty-First Century need to accommodate an ever more sophisticated and educated workforce. Positive Thinking has become management's tool of choice to enable it to hang onto the 1800's mentality while appearing to accommodate the mindset of the Twenty-First Century.

American industry has seen one product line after another go to foreign manufacturers. This did not happen because the foreigners produced a better product. Nor did it happen because of "bad times." It happened (and continues to happen) because the foreign company understood the market better and reacted to it properly. The automobile is a classic example. Detroit was still building its oversized, over-chromed jukeboxes in the gas-starved 1970s when the Japanese took the market away by offering a product people wanted. I find it hard to believe that *no one* in Detroit saw this coming—but there are few people who appreciate change less than executive management, and they made the bad decision to ignore the warning signs—to the applause of their "team players".

Implementing change requires personal strength and the ability to admit that you either don't completely understand something, or may have made a mistake. It takes *character* to face these issues, as well as a willingness to not only use the word No from time to time, but to occasionally hear someone say "No," also.

I sincerely believe that the greatest contribution anyone can ever make in our society is to kill a bad idea with a well-placed *No!* When this privilege is supported, better products will emerge at a faster pace and everyone will come out a winner. When this power is curtailed, everyone loses, because stupidity and inefficiency are given the freedom to grow and to flourish.

✦ ✦ ✦

Despite the obvious example of our own society, there is a general belief in the world of business that dictatorship is more efficient than democracy because, "things get done." This only appears to be true, however. The real world doesn't work that way. Supreme, unquestioned power enables a leader to implement bad as well as good decisions. Whether the decision is to invade a neighboring country or bring out a product that won't sell, unbridled power gives a leader full authority to be wrong. Dictatorships are built on the false assumption that the leader will consistently be right, but this has yet to be the case—in politics or business. Dictators are destroyed because their natural appetites and weaknesses eventually sour the trampled masses, who want and need a better life. The Soviet Union is an excellent political example; K-Mart, which is in the throes of dying due to Wal-Mart's excellent competition, is a good business example.

Another danger of absolute power is its need for total, unquestioning loyalty. Rather than selecting a qualified staff on the basis of ability, the strong man surrounds himself with toadies, people who will do his every bidding. Therefore, the implementation of his ideas (even the good ones) will be second rate. If I were put into a position of political power, I would much rather have a Rush Limbaugh or a Barry Goldwater questioning my every move than a Hermann Goering telling me I am a genius.

Democracy seems inherently inefficient because a plan must be drawn from the cacophony of the many, but it contains a built-in mechanism to destroy bad ideas—*it demands that the good and the bad be given an equal hearing.* Because of this, even the good ideas have a devil of a time making it through to fruition, but the sacrifice is worth the gain. Look at it as a tradeoff. It's far better to kill a bad idea than to implement a good one. So in the long run, we all benefit in some way from the strangulation of red tape—unbelievable as that might sound.

In terms of business, a leader who is empowered to do what he wants, without opposition, runs the danger of making catastrophic mistakes. I realize that by its nature, business is not a democracy—nor should it be. But there must be opposition—a little bit of democracy. Leaders who will not tolerate the word No are on an inevitable path to destruction, and unfortunately, they'll take a lot of us with them.

The Power of NO

> Don't waste time feeling sorry for
> yourself. Spend it constructively.
> Say "No" to the one who stuck it
> to you.

At first the above statement sounds a little vengeful, until you realize that getting back at the people who've been plaguing you all these years involves nothing more than rejecting them—putting them out of your life so that you can enjoy your days more fully. Does such an act give you cause to gloat? Probably. But after a lifetime of unhappiness, you deserve to find pleasure in what you've achieved.

An old business axiom states: *whenever we make a presentation, we tell our audience what we're going to tell them, then we tell them what we came to tell them, then we wrap up by telling them what we told them.* This is the chapter where I *tell* you what I've *told* you—and give you a few more examples for the road.

Learn to Say "No!"

By now you've learned that there is an entire world of people and institutions that are willing to use and abuse our willingness to sacrifice ourselves. They'll take advantage of the fact that we were trained away from the word No at an early age. In fact they depend on it! The only way we can break this chain of abusive self-sacrifice and reject the unhappy elements of our lives is to develop a familiarity—a comfortable working relationship—with the word No. Hopefully, this word will now form the cornerstone of your thought processes. Keep in mind, it should not stop you from well-considered acts of generosity or charity, but it should be the defensive barrier that saves you from other people's thought-less, and at times even cruel, demands.

I suggest that you stand in front of a mirror and watch yourself as you repeat the word softly, then with vigor. Say it rapidly or slowly with feeling, then top it off with a drill-sergeant crescendo. Let it roll as a thundering paean to the heavens. You might even work it into a musical form, or possibly give a cheer: "Gimme an 'N,' Gimme an 'O'! What's it spell?! *Noooooooo!*"

The word must come out flowingly, or as Hamlet said, "trippingly on the tongue." It must come from the depths of your soul and emerge as easily and naturally as a cough or a sneeze. It must be said without hesitation and without qualification—which means with no excuses.

Does it make you feel foolish to say "No"? Does it make you feel uncomfortable? The whole point of your childhood training was to instill these feelings in you. But by now you've learned to weed them out. The word No is not a bad word, it's a tool. And you can either use it to protect yourself, or forego its use and suffer the consequences.

It isn't necessary to say "No" curtly, offensively, or with anger (unless, of course, the situation demands it). However, when you choose to use it, it must be said with finality: with the assurance that it will never be retracted and the confidence that it will never need repeating. This is probably the hardest part of all. Once spoken, it must be cast in concrete, eternal.

The Sales Resistance Formula

Many people who have trouble saying "No" find themselves buying things they really don't want because an aggressive salesperson (or a friend, relative, coworker, or boss) has worn them down. In some cases, a product is actually purchased out of fear or desperation. The customer may have been cowed and intimidated by the salesperson—which is what successful salespeople train themselves to do. This is an excellent arena to practice in, because sales resistance is often the key to developing a mastery of the magic word No. Trust me when I say you are now learning at the knee of the master, because there's little doubt that I have more sales resistance than anyone now breathing on this planet. The more a salesperson insists that I buy a product or service, the greater my resolve not to. Cold, steely resolve is a strong defense and if the battle has gone on long enough, a flash of anger is a fitting coup de grâce to end it.

Don't let the various techniques of trained salespeople convince you that it's wrong to say "No." Some sales people will go so low as to challenge your adequacy as a provider, suggesting that your unwillingness to purchase their product is somehow a violation of your responsibilities.

"But you need more life insurance to protect your family!" they claim.

Wrong!

Others will suggest that you're obligated to help them by buying from them.

"I'm down on my luck and good Christians must buy my magazine subscription to help me get back on my feet!"

Wrong again!

Remember, you don't owe anything to a stranger soliciting at your door. If the magazine isn't something you want, say "No," and don't buy it.

I offer here the *Sales Resistance Formula,* which can be stated simply as $P = R + 1$. In other words, pressure (P) must always be met by an equal amount of resistance (R) plus one additional unit of force. As the pressure increases, so must the resistance, so we could easily write the equation as $P^3 = R^3 + 1$ (always one unit of force ahead). This is not unlike the mechanical rabbit at the dog track that's always a bit faster than the fastest dog. If you follow this formula by using the word No as your means of resistance, you will never—repeat, *never*—buy anything you don't want again.

Now you understand why I advocate sales resistance as a means of practicing your ability to say "No." It's good to start with door-to-door salespeople because of the security of operating on your own turf. When your skills and resolve have improved, you can go into their lair—an insurance office, for example—and practice holding out. The final test, and the one that only real pros dare tackle, is a big automobile dealership. By *big,* I mean one that frequently advertises (especially on television) and employs a small army of cannibals who live by jumping on someone's flesh and not letting go until that person signs some papers (especially leases— they love the leases). I've been through this routine on numerous occasions in Los Angeles where no quarter is given, and I can see how it might be a frightening experience for anyone who has trouble saying "No" on a far less-intensive level than a car dealership.

As I said before, this is the supreme test. It probably isn't a necessity for anyone who merely wants to obtain the amount of practice requisite for daily living, but it's something to shoot for— like getting an advanced degree at a university—and it certainly can do a lot to build your confidence. Anyone who can make it through the minefield of a major car dealership is well prepared for any eventuality. Even a brother-in-law asking for a handout is like a parlor game to someone who has experience swimming with the sharks.

The Power of the Word

No is easily the most powerful word in the English language. I personally believe it is the greatest force for good in the entire lexicon—and I can think of no better morale builder. People who consistently cave in under pressure never feel good about themselves. Giving "another chance" to someone who doesn't deserve it usually leaves the "giver" feeling obligated to defend the position. However, standing up for yourself (indeed for what's *right*) and saying "No," is an experience not unlike being reborn.

Several years ago, a very misunderstood First Lady was ridiculed without mercy for her *Just Say No* solution to the drug problem. Those precious few who stopped to consider the statement seriously, however, quickly realized that Nancy Reagan was absolutely *right*. In real life, the user has the choice of either saying "No" or eventually giving a last breath for a fix.

Alcoholics can join a support group, undergo psychoanalysis, try hypnosis, try religion, or even quit cold turkey on their own. In the final analysis, however, it all comes down to the same unavoidable conclusion. The alcoholic must choose to quit drinking. The alcoholic, like the drug addict, must say "No." This is not an oversimplification; it is an eternal and undeniable truth. The solution to alcoholism or drug addiction is to *quit*. The word No can quite literally save people's lives.

It's Okay to Say "No"

All of the people mentioned in this book had to say "No" to someone or something in order to make their lives happier. Nora had to back off and let Bill handle Daphne. Art and Marilyn had to stand up to their relatives in Wisconsin. Leslie had to face a situation that wasn't going to correct itself and leave her husband. These people all said "No"—perhaps a bit late in some cases—but they all said it, nonetheless, and were immeasurably better off for doing it.

Somewhere along the line we were taught that it's bad to be negative. If you believe this, ask yourself where always saying "yes" has taken you. To be forever self-sacrificing is to allow people to walk all over you, and there's absolutely no justification for this. Conscientious self-sacrifice is noble. Meaningless self-sacrifice is self-destructive. Even the Bible doesn't teach that we should be forever self-sacrificing, but that everything should be done in a "fitting and orderly way."

Let me tell you about Myrna. I would like to say she was a friend, but I never actually met the lady. She was a friend of my grandparents, something of a legend in our family, and she passed away when I was very young. Myrna was the only girl and next to the youngest in a family of five children. The family lived on a farm in upstate New York, somewhere in the vicinity of Syracuse. Myrna's mother died when Myrna was about thirteen, and it was "decided" that she would take over all duties as homemaker, which was generally accepted as being "woman's work." She would do all of the cooking, cleaning, ironing, and laundry, all with no help from her father or brothers. She somehow made it through high school and then decided she was going to college. Of course, this idea was met with total resistance by all five males, who apparently couldn't fry an egg, much less wash a shirt, and she was told in no uncertain terms that she was not going to leave home and go traipsing off to college. Her job was to stay home and look after her father and brothers. They needed a drudge, and Myrna had been elected in a landslide victory.

What they didn't know was that Myrna was an excellent student and had applied for a college scholarship. Indeed, the scholarship had already been granted—a completely free ride through a major university. She left home despite the objections and went on to earn both a bachelor's degree and a master's degree. Eventually, she moved to the West Coast, started her own business, and died a half-century later as a wealthy and respected lady. It can be assumed that somewhere along the line, the male members of her family learned how to put a peanut-butter sandwich together and survived.

I heard this story of Myrna and her accomplishments many times while I was growing up, but it was only a few years ago that I learned the story of her departure, and this is the part of the story that is relevant to us. It seems that during the week before she left for the university, her father and brothers quit speaking to her. Instead of feeling proud that she had run a large household as a teenager and still found the time and determination to win a scholarship, they felt betrayed. After all, they had put a roof over her head, let her eat at their table, and furnished her with an endless supply of laundry to fill her empty hours.

No one said goodbye when Myrna left. No one offered to take her to the railroad station. She did pin a note to the front door when she left that said, "All of you—go to hell." From there, it was off to a world of higher learning and financial success.

As I think about Myrna and her message, I detect a lot of anguish, some frustration, and obviously no small amount of hatred (understandable, given the circumstances). But like all of us, she had to make a choice in her life. She could say "Yes" and continue in her misery, or say "No" and gain control of her life. In my opinion, she did the right thing. The message she left pinned to the front door of her father's home was inspired, and I think that any browbeaten and ill-used teenager who can work up the spirit to leave such a message has the stuff of success in abundant amounts.

✦ ✦ ✦

The next time a pack of distant relatives asks to drain your bank account to pay for their bad decisions, you could do a lot worse than to remember Myrna and the words of a tortured, teenage girl who became a mature woman in a matter of seconds.

However, the most important thing to remember is that Myrna never regretted what she did, and neither does anyone else who gathers the courage for a sincere and necessary write-off. She said "No" to the whole family and went on to do what she had every right to do.

I suggest you try it once. I guarantee you'll try it again.

Random Thoughts to Get You Through the Day

When someone says that he will call you right back, assume that he won't. This is the cornerstone of all human relations.

It's better to be bitter and vengeful than too stupid to realize that it's the way you should feel.

Never underestimate the simpleton. Stupid people are often the most treacherous of all.

When in doubt, say "No." To say that something won't work, won't happen, or won't be accepted is a much safer bet than saying that it will.

If you have nothing that anyone wants, you can afford to love mankind and trust your fellow human beings. Otherwise, don't sit with your back to the door.

People who borrow money from friends seem to be capable of only two emotions: groveling obeisance when they seek the loan, and indignation when they're asked to pay it back.

It is not always beneficial to hear the other fellow's point of view. If he is an obvious jackass, there is little to be gained from his recital of misinformation and illogical conclusions.

Those who owe us money can be very difficult to contact. The best way to communicate with them is by having a pack of angry dogs run them up a tree.

Most of our problems can be solved by the simple measure of having someone stop doing something.

No one has ever been disappointed by someone he didn't trust in the first place.

Those who would presume to remake the world are invariably the ones with the most difficulty replacing the eraser in the mechanical pencil.

Diplomacy is a device to give the contestants something to do until they're ready to fight, not unlike skipping rope in the dressing room.

A problem is solved only when the person with the ability to solve it wants it to be solved. Until this happens, nothing is produced but a lot of noise.

The man who craves power usually shouldn't have it, and the man who can handle it usually doesn't want it. This is the great dilemma of history.

Incompetence in command may not be the greatest of all human sins, but it is assuredly the most inexcusable.

A formal wedding is a prime example of man's indefatigable ability to complicate even the simplest of issues.

Please don't tell me about the brotherhood of man. I know several people whom I wouldn't accept as distant cousins.

Human progress is destined to be eternally retarded by man's insatiable passion for marching in ranks behind the banner of an imbecile.

It isn't all that difficult to make a major contribution to the betterment of mankind. Anyone who isn't serving on a committee is helping immeasurably.

The word *activist* was coined by journalists to give them a single word to describe someone with a big mouth and no apparent job, skills, or credentials.

Donald G. Smith is an advocate for the millions of people who suffer daily from the onslaught of moochers who want to take them for every dime in their pockets, usurp every second of their lives, and strain every ounce of their sanity. His goal is to help people learn that with a little practice, they can be free of these leeches and live happier lives.

More than twenty years of work as an editor and editorial supervisor in the aerospace industry have taught Smith that having the strength to choose *how* you live can greatly enhance your quality of life. He has shared his experiences on many radio talk shows and through the messages of his books: *How to Cure Yourself of Positive Thinking, The Joy of Negative Thinking, People I Could Do Without, Common Sense for the Beginner, Now Hear This,* and *It's OK to Say NO.*

Smith and his wife Eileen live in Santa Maria, California, and he's very proud of his son, David, who hosts a sports-radio talk show in Los Angeles. He likes all sports (especially college football), jazz, dogs, vodka martinis, maps, corduroy, and Winslow Homer. His favorite cities are San Francisco and Atlanta, and he regards Winston Churchill as the greatest human being of his time. Smith is also the founder of a writers' support group in Santa Maria where he teaches adult writing courses and helps anyone who asks learn how to slam the door in the faces of their own Problem Perennials.